Empowerment and Social Work Participation

Empowerment and Social Work Participation

Savita Bhatt

ADHYAYAN

ADHYAYAN PUBLISHERS & DISTRIBUTORS

NEW DELHI (INDIA)

Published by
ADHYAYAN PUBLISHERS & DISTRIBUTORS
4378/4B, 105, J.M.D. House, Murari Lal Street
Ansari Road Darya Ganj, New Delhi - 110002
Ph.: 011-23263018, 011-23277156, Fax: 011-23280028
Email: adhyayanpublishers@yahoo.com

Empowerment and Social Work Participation

Edition 2010
ISBN 978-81-8435-223-8

Printed in India

Published by Harish Chandra Yadav for Adhyayan Publishers & Distributors, Laser Typeseting at A.V. Rao and Printed at Tarun Offset Printers, Delhi

Preface

The concept of "empowerment" has been accepted widely in recent years and now is used extensively in the field of social work. This approach, which first developed in the 1970s, increasingly is used in welfare policy, social programs, or direct intervention, and it replaces the traditional therapist-client model of the helping relationship. Over the years, the empowerment concept has taken shape and acquired meaning primarily through the work of social theorists, rather than practitioners or consumers of services.

Social workers with only an individualistic understanding of empowerment will easily end up as moralising agents rather than as facilitators for their clients. It is in the complex interaction between a given socio-material situation and the individual capacity to interpret and act that one finds the key to an empowerment worthy of its name. This presupposes two things: that social workers have as a part of their education theoretical knowledge about organisational structures, and that they themselves have been empowered in ways that give them practical competence to act in relation to situations. They need the competence to identify the complexities of interests and power relations in society.

This book offers coverage that spans both conceptual debates about empowerment and the range of practice issues and challenges that face a social work audience today. It provides a rigorous discussion of theory, drawing on global aspects of empowerment and linking this clearly to the needs of service users. Proper emphasis is also given to clarity of style and accessibility so that the book continues to offer an essential resource at all levels of study. Covering a broad range of core topics, the book is suitable for undergraduate students in sociology, psychology and other fields of social science.

Author

Contents

1

Introduction

The term *empowerment* refers to increasing the spiritual, political, social, or economic strength of individuals and communities. It often involves the empowered developing confidence in their own capacities. The term covers a vast landscape of meanings, interpretations, definitions and disciplines ranging from psychology and philosophy to the highly commercialized self-help industry and motivational sciences.Sociological empowerment often addresses members of groups that social discrimination processes have excluded from decision-making processes through - for example - discrimination based on disability, race, ethnicity, religion, or gender. Empowerment as a methodology is often associated with feminism: see consciousness-raising.

Rmpowermenting the Marginalized Society

Marginalized refers to the overt or covert trends within societies whereby those perceived as lacking desirable traits or deviating from the group norms tend to be excluded by wider society and ostracised as undesirables. Sometimes groups are marginalized by society at large, but governments are often unwitting or enthusiastic participants. For example, the U.S. government marginalized cultural minorities, particularly blacks, prior to the Civil Rights Act of 1964. This Act made it illegal to restrict access to schools and public places based on race. Equal opportunity laws which actively oppose such marginalization, allow increased empowerment to occur. It should be noted that they are also a symptom of minorities' and women's empowerment through lobbying.

Marginalized people who have no opportunities for self-sufficiency become, at a minimum, dependent on charity or welfare. They lose their self-confidence because they cannot be fully self-supporting. The opportunities denied them also deprive them of the pride of accomplishment which others, who have those opportunities, can develop for themselves. This in turn can lead to psychological, social and even mental health problems.

Empowerment is then the process of obtaining these basic opportunities for marginalized people, either directly by those people, or through the help of non-marginalized others who share their own access to these opportunities. It also includes actively thwarting attempts to deny those opportunities. Empowerment also includes encouraging, and developing the skills for, self-sufficiency, with a focus on eliminating the future need for charity or welfare in the individuals of the group. This process can be difficult to start and to implement effectively, but there are many examples of empowerment projects which have succeeded.

One empowerment strategy is to assist marginalized people to create their own nonprofit organization, using the rationale that only the marginalized people, themselves, can know what their own people need most, and that control of the organization by outsiders can actually help to further entrench marginalization. Charitable organizations lead from outside of the community, for example, can disempower the community by entrenching a dependence on charity or welfare. A nonprofit organization can target strategies that cause structural changes, reducing the need for ongoing dependence. Red Cross, for example, can focus on improving the health of indigenous people, but does not have authority in its charter to install water-delivery and purification systems, even though the lack of such a system profoundly, directly and negatively impacts health. A nonprofit composed of the indigenous people, however, could insure their own organization does have such authority and could set their own agendas, make their own plans, seek the needed resources, do as much of the work as they can, and take responsibility - and credit - for the success of their projects.

Numerous critical perspectives exist that propose that an empowerment paradigm is present, Clark showed that whilst there was a degree of autonomy provided by empowerment, it also made way for extended surveillance and control, hence the contradiction perspective.

PROCESS OF EMPOWERMENT

The process which enables individuals/groups to fully access personal/collective power, authority and influence, and to employ that strength when engaging with other people, institutions or society.

Empowerment includes the following, or similar, capabilities:-

— The ability to make decisions about personal/collective circumstances
— The ability to access information and resources for decision-making
— Ability to consider a range of options from which to choose (not just yes/no, either/or.)
— Ability to exercise assertiveness in collective decision making
— Having positive-thinking about the ability to make change
— Ability to learn and access skills for improving personal/ collective circumstance.
— Ability to inform others' perceptions though exchange, education and engagement.
— Involving in the growth process and changes that is never ending and self-initiated
— Increasing one's positive self-image and overcoming stigma
— Increasing one's ability in discreet thinking to sort out right and wrong

Workplace Empowerment

One account of the history of workplace empowerment in the United States recalls the clash of management styles in railroad construction in the American West in the mid-19th century, where "traditional" hierarchical East-Coast models of control encountered individualistic pioneer workers, strongly supplemented by methods of efficiency-oriented "worker responsibility" brought to the scene by Chinese laborers. In this case, empowerment at the level of work teams or brigades achieved a notable (but short-lived) demonstrated superiority.

Empowerment in the workplace is regarded by critics as more a pseudo-empowerment exercise, the idea of which is to change the attitudes of workers, so as to make them work harder rather than giving them any real power, and Wilkinson refers to this as "attitudinal shaping". However, recent research suggests that the opportunity to exercise personal discretion/choice (and complete meaningful work) is an important element contributing to employee engagement and well-being. There is evidence that initiative and motivation are increased when people have a more positive attributional style. This influences self-belief, resilience when faced with setbacks, and the ability to visualize oneself overcoming problems. The implication is that 'empowerment' suits some more than others, and should be positioned in the broader and wider context of an 'enabling' work environment.

Empowerment to employees in the work place provides them with opportunities to make their own decisions with regards to their tasks. Now-a-days more and more bosses and managers are practicing the concept of empowerment among their subordinates to provide them with better opportunities.

Economics and Empowerment

In economic development, the empowerment approach focuses on mobilizing the self-help efforts of the poor, rather than providing them with social welfare. Economic empowerment is also the empowering of previously disadvantaged sections of the population, for example, in many previously colonized African countries.

Personal Development and Empowerment

In the arena of personal development, empowerment forms an apogee of many a system of Self Realization or of identity (re-)formation. Realizing the solipsistic impracticality of everyone anarchistically attempting to exercise power over everyone else, empowerment advocates have adopted the word "empowerment" to offer the attractions of such power, but they generally constrain its individual exercise to potentiality and to feel-good uses within the individual psyche. The concept of personal development is seen as important by many employers, with emphasis placed on continuous learning, increased self-awareness and emotional intelligence. Empowerment is ultimately driven by the individual's belief in their capability to influence events.

Empowerment can be attained through one or many ways. An important factor in the discovery and application of the human "self empowerment" lies within the tools used to unveil the truth. It has been suggested that Yoga is one such tool that can be used for more than the obvious physical benefits. When Yoga is practiced consistently the mind / body connection is apparent. Through this connection, the individual finds him or herself with a stronger sense of self and the ability to change areas where bad habits rule, negative emotions run rampant, even controlling addictions through understanding them for what they are. What can be more empowering than gaining control over self.

Empowerment via Social Work

The concept of "empowerment" has been accepted widely in recent years and now is used extensively in the field of social work. This approach, which first developed in the 1970s, increasingly is used in welfare policy, social programs, or direct intervention, and it replaces the traditional therapist-client model of the helping relationship.

Over the years, the empowerment concept has taken shape and acquired meaning primarily through the work of social theorists, rather than practitioners or consumers of services. The process of theory development has been deductive and top-down rather than inductive and bottom-up.

It should be noted that there is disagreement and debate about the most empowering term to denote the individuals who are served or assisted by social work professionals. A variety of terms, including "clients," "customers," "users," and consumers," all have been used, and each in turn has been criticized for being inadequate in some respect. Recognizing this problem, we have chosen to use the term "consumer". Although the word leaves much to be desired, in our judgment, it is the most widely accepted term by those wishing to use language that reflects empowering relationships.

The concept of "power" goes to the heart of empowerment theory. Lukes described two aspects of power: "power to" and "power over. The "power to" involves an individual's ability to act efficaciously to bring about desired results. Such capability is central to the meaning of empowerment; and the kinds of experiences, competences and skills necessary to actualize empowerment is a consistent theme in the literature about this concept. Much of the literature deals with components and subelements of personal empowerment, such as self-efficacy, self-esteem, mastery, perceived competence, and assertiveness. The development of consciousness-raising and critical thinking abilities also is a common theme, as is building knowledge, capacities and skills.

On the other hand, Lukes asserted that "A exercises power over B when A affects B in a manner contrary to B's interests". However, there is much disagreement about how power is exercised and what constitutes people's interests. Those from a pluralist perspective have focused on contested interests and the manner in which decisions are made). Others have called attention to a second, hidden dimension—the ability to control the realization of interests by preventing decisions from being made or the nonuse of power by elites to prevent social conflicts and to preserve social order. Still others have explored the construction of power combining both personal and social dimensions or the "real interests" which may not even be perceived by B because A is able to construct and define social reality.

This conceptualization of power is relational, and empowerment refers to processes and outcomes whereby less powerful individuals and groups move to reduce discrepancies in power relationships either through zero-sum, win-lose strategies or mutual benefit, win-win approaches. For example, Rubenstein and Lawler submitted that empowerment should be viewed through connections and mutually empathic relations. They suggested that personal empowerment and the relational context through which it emerges must be considered simultaneously. Zimmerman, Israel, Schultz, and Checkoway identified an interactional component of empowerment that refers to the connections and transactions between people and environments that lead to successful mastery of social systems. Additional studies stress group empowerment or collective empowerment or explore different aspects of community, organizational, and political empowerment.

Social Work and Social Empowerment

Social workers have an enormously difficult task. Social services departments have now abandoned any pretence of open-door, community-based services to individuals and families. Their resources are so very tightly controlled that only those with the greatest needs receive services. Some clients are therefore reduced to outpourings of rage and anger to get heard. Dealing with the impact of poverty and structural inequality is central to the social work role. Social workers must recognise the effects of widening inequality over the past twenty years and challenge this trend. Unless social workers use their powers creatively to bring about practical improvements in the lives of their clients they cannot claim to be any more than gatekeepers of resources, or social policemen. In some deprived communities social work is already seen as a form of oppression against the poor.

Very often the fast-track route to services for children in need is through the child protection system. With a little imagination it is often possible to redefine needs so that they fit into a category for child protection registration. Families are manoeuvred into situations where they have to demonstrate that they have failed in some way or that relationships have completely broken down before resources are made available to them. Consequently, child protection social workers spend much of their time policing the parenting of extremely disadvantaged people who need services more than surveillance. Social workers are aware that the risks allegedly posed by these parents would disappear if they had the resources of a more privileged family. Social workers should not lose sight of their broader social objectives. They should resist pressures to deal with clients in a narrowly legalistic and depersonalised way. At the same time social workers, their clients and the wider community need to work together in demanding adequate resources from the state for vulnerable individuals and families.

The new social work degree will make entry into the profession more difficult for working class people. This is another example of the way that class discrimination is gradually seeping into the profession.Support for the social work degree clearly comes from the middle classes. The belief that social workers need longer basic training is an implied criticism of them and affirmation of the value of training. This has come about largely through an alliance between middle class managers, academics and politicians.

A key philosophical issue in social work is the nature of the relationship between the individual and the state. Social work seeks to establish the right balance between respecting privacy and intervening to provide care and control. The working class regards social work as part of the controlling state. However, social work trainers who are predominantly middle class, stress the caring aspect of the social work role and teach anti-oppressive practice. Consequently, newly-qualified social workers are ill-prepared for the job because the values they have been taught during training do not fit with those underpinning service delivery. These problems can only be addressed if class is put at the centre of training. Class must be discussed and thought about more clearly. Anti-oppressive practice must be taught in a way that includes getting to grips with class oppression. Unless social workers have a realistic class analysis they may unwittingly succumb to pressures to behave oppressively.

Social Work for Poverty Eradication

One of the most serious problems affecting the health and well-being of many social work clients is poverty. Poverty is not just about income but also the quality of life and the home and community environment. However, social services departments construct needs in ways that ignore needs arising out of poverty. The reason must be that poverty is perceived as something about which social services can do nothing. The links between poverty and health problems are well known. Poverty and illness together make people much more vulnerable and needy at all stages of their lives, and even more so in old age. Inequalities between social classes in the incidence of chronic illness and mental illness and in life expectancy are also well documented.

Social work may endorse anti-oppressive ideas but class inequalities remain as wide as ever. Clearly, anti-oppressive practice is at its weakest when it comes to the issue of class. Moral judgements about worth and deservedness permeate social work practice and unthinking class assumptions continue to influence the provision of services. For example, social work assessments inevitably include considerations of how well poor clients are dealing with their poverty. Furthermore, when social work decisions are challenged the more powerful and articulate middle classes are more likely to be successful in getting the services they need than the less powerful working classes.

The government assumes that social workers can deal with poverty without tackling the underlying causes. It continuously repeats the mantra of education as a panacea for all poverty and inequality. In reality, social workers can do nothing about raising household incomes, improving housing or transforming the community environment. Social workers must therefore resist the notion that poverty can be tackled by apolitical social work solutions.

Social workers have a responsibility to work towards structural change to resolve the issues their clients face which are caused by inequalities of income and wealth. It is not enough to simply resolve individual issues as they arise. The social work profession promotes social change, problem solving in human relationships and the empowerment and liberation of people to enhance well-being. Utilising theories of human behaviour and social systems, social work intervenes at the points where people interact with their environments.

In recent years, the language of poverty and inequality has been replaced by that of social exclusion. This has been introduced to disguise the true extent of poverty and to create the illusion that the problem is being tackled. This process inevitably requires the poor to be blamed for their poverty. It involves the mindless repetition of words and phrases that have lost any connection with meanings - equality of opportunity, inclusiveness, stakeholder - and the avoidance of any embarrassing facts about poverty. Public perception of poverty is manipulated so that the better-off do not have to take any responsibility for the problem. Meanwhile, poverty remains as serious a problem as ever.

Even the social work profession has become involved in this false way of thinking. The 'official' language sweeps away principles of social justice and any notion that social workers should be aligned with poor, working class people. The 'correct' view is that the social worker is simply employed to mediate between the client and the state and this can be achieved without any reference to poverty, inequality and class. Academics, too, are uncritically promoting the 'official' language. They are writing more and more in an artificial language that cuts them off from the real world. Their language is becoming so dense and convoluted that it is either incomprehensible or meaningless. They appear too eager to follow the lead of politicians - who are renowned for their manipulation of language and their concern with spin.

The 'official' language plays down the significance of power and class differentials between clients and social workers. It denies the reality of statutory social work where the struggle for power and control characterises much interaction with clients. It is designed to ensure that clients are groomed and moulded into the official system and that conflict is avoided.

In both child welfare and mental health services new strategies are emerging which have as their focus the assessment and management of risk and a clearer duty to share confidential information. As social workers are seen as carrying out surveillance and monitoring activities on behalf of the state, their clients, who are predominantly poor and working class, are becoming increasingly alienated from them. In this climate it is remarkable that there are still some social workers who are concerned with tackling the effects of poverty and who succeed in finding ways to meet their clients' financial needs. These are often social workers who have been influenced by their own experiences of poverty. They tend to have a broader view of the social work task and to be committed to principles of social welfare and justice.

Clients coming into the orbit of social services are sometimes people who have been pushed into poverty by a personal crisis and unemployment and need information about their entitlement to benefits and advice about debt problems. However, providing help with financial matters is generally given low priority. It is now policy in many departments that social workers do not deal with income maintenance issues if they can refer clients to voluntary agencies which provide welfare rights advice and advocacy. Meanwhile, there is a sense of crisis in the profession. Many of the problems have been brought about by the government and its obsession with performance targets which creates the illusion that something is being done when in reality the situation is getting worse. It is nonsense to suggest that targets are achievable if management has no understanding of the complexity of the problems that social workers address and the barriers to their meeting the real needs of people they purport to help.

Any credible analysis of poverty must reflect the class divisions in society which give rise to, and perpetuate, inequalities of income and wealth. Social work cannot be expected to have an impact on the consequential problems unless the root causes of poverty are honestly acknowledged and addressed.

Social Work for Child Protection

Politicians often choose to present child protection as part of social care, and as a social work service, but this is misleading. Social work intervention in child protection matters is quite different from social care. Child protection social workers face difficult ethical issues. The service has a social control function and even those children helped by child protection seem reluctant clients. Research shows that much child protection work does not get to grips with the underlying causes of maltreatment, nor compensate for the harm done to the child. Its effectiveness lies in its powers to separate the child from harmful parents and to carry out monitoring and surveillance activities. The primary aims of child protection are child rescue and the policing of families.

Social workers in child protection are allowed to survive to the extent that they perform a function for governments in managing and controlling disadvantaged and oppressed people. They have been reduced to policing families because this is the only secure role for them.The child protection service normally concentrates on those cases that are inherently severe and on incidents widely accepted as being abusive. Cases which need family support services and where the children are likely to come from the most impoverished and deprived sections of the community are better dealt with by a less stigmatising service.Social work intervention in families is driven by departmental procedures which are more concerned with systems for investigation than strategies for intervention.

In the past, good child care practice accepted the inherent tension between care and control and was supported by an organisational structure and practice which integrated both aspects. However, over the past decade the statutory services have undergone profound change.One of the effects of this has been the administrative separation of caring activities from controlling activities. When this happens the child protection service becomes transformed into a "social policing" service, no longer informed by the principles and values of good social work practice.

To argue that child protection is not social work is to present a challenge to the profession. It raises questions about the need for a professional code of ethics in child protection work. The current modernising agenda is already taking the debate about the future of social work away from values towards performance and outcome measures. Child protection workers and training establishments need to face up to these issues so students are better prepared for the realities of the job. It is pointless teaching students about empowerment and advocacy if social work is essentially about social control.

The history of child care and child protection work has not been one of continuous progress. A recurring theme throughout the past fifty years has been the struggle to achieve an appropriate balance between care and control. During the past two decades social policy has shifted the balance towards control and local authorities have become more concerned with policing child abuse and neglect than with caring for vulnerable children and families.

Child protection social workers may have the skills to work supportively but their role is essentially coercive. They are expected to act decisively to protect children from abuse and neglect and, if their intervention is occasionally brutal and heavy-handed, this is seen as unavoidable. It means that social workers are generally given a free rein to behave oppressively because we are all in favour of the protection of children. Unfortunately, many middle class social workers are blind to the processes within their own organisation which oppress the working class. For example, so-called 'family support services' are stigmatising because they are generally directed at those families which are poor, disadvantaged and vulnerable; the class system operates to protect the more powerful, privileged and better-off families from social work intervention. And any services provided are usually the 'carrot' used to persuade families to accept the 'stick' of social work surveillance and monitoring. Significantly, the services provided rarely include respite care or home help, the ones most often requested by parents under stress.

Despite all the rhetoric of 'family support' many local authorities do not have the staff or the resources to provide this. Furthermore, because local authorities now provide an explicit child protection service, families do not approach them for support. Even families on the receiving end of child protection 'services' are reluctant to ask for help as their social worker may use this as evidence against them. While managers may claim to have policies combining supportive services with child protection, in practice it is the social workers who are expected to achieve this on their own. It often seems an impossible task and that is why many good social workers are leaving their jobs.

The current crisis in child protection work has arisen because it has moved in the wrong direction and much of the work is now of a 'hit or miss' nature. Child protection social workers, being at the centre of many conflicting pressures and influences, are uncertain of their role and therefore tend to fall back on their own moral judgements. Inevitably, this means that class prejudices operate and that poor, working class people are sometimes treated unfairly.

A possible solution is to create an administrative separation of the 'policing' function and the 'social work' function. Investigations of child abuse should be the function of a separate agency which would make an initial assessment and then determine the action required from other services. The new agency would only deal with those cases which are inherently severe and self-evidently abusive. It should be recognised as a 'policing' service and primarily concerned with the enforcement of the law to protect children from abuse.

Cases which are not so clear-cut, such as most cases of neglect and emotional abuse, and where the children are likely to come from the most marginalised and deprived sections of the community, would be dealt with by a family support service, based on traditional social work values. The emphasis would be on the social worker working with vulnerable parents and children over a long period of time and getting close enough for open and honest discussions. The family support service would need to develop its own practice frameworks to help with the difficult task of balancing risks and responsibilities and the experience of family centres, particularly those based on the neighbourhood model, would be very useful.

The current drive to increase professional training as a way of solving these organisational problems is misguided. There is no shortage of people with relevant experiences, who have a real feeling for others and are committed to working to improve the lives of the poor and disadvantaged. What these people need is not more qualifications but new structures for working creatively in their own communities.

The organisation of child protection work needs to undergo radical change. Social work already has much to offer in understanding and tackling the problems of deprivation and poverty - which are at the centre of much child and family work. It is time to create a new structure for social work activity that has the vision and commitment to making real improvements in the lives of poor children and families living in deprived communities. The welfare of children 'in need' is too important to be tacked on to the workload of under-staffed, over-burdened child protection teams.

Role of Social Workers in Promoting Breastfeeding

The most important form of infant nutrition is breastfeeding. Unfortunately there has been a steady decline in breast-feeding practices in the post-industrialized era. Breast milk substitutes, a major threat to breast-feeding, are indeed a big business. The invasion of the markets with a product seeking to substitute nature's gift to the new born child evoked public resentment in the form of various campaigns. While this has been the visible context of the campaign for the promotion of breast-feeding in India there are several other socio-cultural practices that interfere with optimal breast-feeding.

Aggressive marketing of breast milk substitutes by commercial interests triggered campaigns for promotion of breast-feeding. Additionally, the promotion of breast milk substitutes by medical professionals challenged traditional breast-feeding practices. The trend is further reinforced by increasing urbanization processes that do not accommodate the needs of the feeding mother and the infant.

With the breakdown of the joint family system, there is an absence of significant other older women in the family who can advise the young mother. This often increases the mother's vulnerability and insecurity in breast-feeding the child.

The pressures of urban life create stress in women, which interferes with breast-feeding. Distance between the workplace of the mother and residence also demands functional adaptations in coping with breast-feeding. For example, where a mother cannot reach the baby during the day while at work, she can express the milk into a clean cup which can be fed later to the child and give more emphasis on night feeding. Increasing hospital deliveries are significantly responsible for decline in breast-feeding where medical personnel do not actively promote breast-feeding, but advocate breast-feeding substitutes instead. Under such circumstances, women are less likely to breast-feed their babies. The baby food industry cleverly sought to promote its products through health care facilities.

An all-India market study by UNICEFACASH revealed that the incidence of free samples prevailed all over India - it was highest in the country's capital, New Delhi, followed by Eastern, Western and Southern India. Seventy-two per cent of the free samples were given by Nestle; other companies being Dalmia Dairy (24 per cent), Wockhardt (19 per cent) and Raptokos Brett (18 per cent). They even sponsored major events for professional medical and nutrition bodies to win their support. Large commercial interests coupled with the teaching of formula milk feeding in medical colleges became major barriers in the promotion of breast-feeding.

The responses of pediatricians, nutritionists, and social scientists to the onslaught of bottle feeding in India, was reflected in the spate of studies on breast-feeding practices and child nutrition in India in the seventies and eighties. These studies provide interesting insights into the socio-cultural aspects of breast-feeding. From the wide range of studies available, it is evident that there is a strong tradition of breast-feeding in India, especially in the rural areas. Simultaneously, a dramatic decline in breast-feeding is well documented in the urban and semi-urban environment.

The rural-urban migration of the poor, the increased interaction of this group with the concomitants of modernization including mass media communication networks, access to job opportunities, commercial products and their availability, set into a process a consumeristic behavior based on imitation rather than need or rational decision-making. An inverse relationship is observed between socioeconomic status and breast-feeding: the lower income groups pay a heavier price from being deprived of breast milk, for they miss the natural immunity it provides. They are vulnerable to infection not just from unhygienic surroundings, but also due to unsterilized bottles and nipples, unpotable water, excessive dilution of formula due to poverty, and illiteracy. Babies that are exclusively breast-fed are less likely to suffer from diarrhea and upper respiratory illnesses. The practice of breast-feeding in addition to satisfying the nutritional needs of the baby also creates a strong mother-child bonding.

Bottle-feeding is a growing phenomenon in rural tribal areas. The bottle feeding culture, though initiated by the power milk industry, is not restricted to feeding powder milk. One can see infants and children being given water, fresh milk, fruit juices and clear soups in feeding bottles. The feeding bottle is an important factor in the infamous malnutrition infection cycle, often reported to be a major cause of infant and child mortality.

With scarcity of water and firewood, it is impossible to expect people to sterilize bottles after each feed. Besides, under all circumstances, cup feeding is more hygienic though bottle-feeding may be more convenient. If mothers are able to meet the hygiene requirements of bottle-feeding, they have a choice to do so, but this should be on an informed basis. They must know that all types of allergy, insulin dependent diabetes mellitis, lymphoma, obesity, sudden infant death syndrome, which are non-infective disorders, are known to increase with bottle feeding.

Appropriate spacing of children has been a crucial concern of the Family Planning Program in India. Studies show that breast-feeding acts as a contraceptive in 98 per cent of women for the first six months, and in 85 to 90 per cent of mothers till they menstruate. These trends invite broader concerns in the breast-feeding promotion campaign in India, besides seeking control over expansion of powder milks, follow-up milks and processed weaning foods.

The campaigns for promotion of breast-feeding arose out of global concern against processed milk substitutes for infants. The

World Health Organization (WHO) and the United Nations International Children's Fund (UNICEF) have played a catalytic role in the campaign through advocacy, information and social mobilization.

During the seventies, several citizens' Groups all over the world started campaigning for controls on advertising and marketing baby foods. In 1972, the International Organization of Consumers Unions (IOCU) submitted a draft code of practice on the advertising of infant foods to FAO/WHO. As the campaign gained momentum, the threat of manufactured breast milk substitutes were taken cognizance of by the WHO and the UNICEF. An international meeting was called 1979 by WHO and UNICEF on infant and young child feeding. Two major outcomes of the meeting were: formation of the International Code of Marketing for Infant Formulae, 1981; and the formation of the International Baby Food Action Network (IBFAN).

The 1981 World Health Assembly adopted the code with an overwhelming majority of 188 to 1 votes. The one dissenting vote was from the United States of America (USA). The possible reason for opposition was the fear of damage to the infant formula companies many of which were in the USA. The code in its entirety was approved as recommendation to all member governments. In 1986, the same Assembly passed a resolution banning, free and subsidized supplies to hospitals and maternity homes and discouraged the use of follow-up formula for children over six months of age. It urged a total ban on donated and subsidized supplies of infant milk powder. At one point, the UNICEF had actively assisted powder milk industries to reestablish themselves after they were destroyed in the Second World War, on the condition that they would provide free or subsidized powder milk to developing countries. Thus with experience, these agencies had to make functional adaptations in policy and program.

In India, active movements were started by voluntary and consumer groups, including the Consumer Guidance Society of India (CGSI) and the Voluntary Health Association of India (VHAI). They formed a network called the National Alliance for the Nutrition of Infants (NANI). With suasion from these groups, the Government of India adopted code in the form of a resolution in December 1983. The Infant Milk Foods and Feeding Bottles Bill was passed in the Lok

Sabha in 1989. It was reintroduced in 1991 but lapsed again for the same reason. In 1992, the 'Infant Milk Substitutes, Feeding Bottles and Infant Foods (Regulation of Production, Supply and Distribution) Act was finally passed. It came into force from August 1, 1993. It prohibits:

— Distribution of free samples to mothers;
-- Advertising to the public;
— Promotion in health care facilities;
— Distribution of gifts or samples to health workers;
— Promotion of words and pictures that idealize bottle feeding;
— Advice to mothers by company sales staff;
— Financial assistance to health organizations or associations of doctors to organize conferences, seminars, and so on; and
— Incentives to sales personnel/retailers based on volume of sales.

The Central Government, has authorized four voluntary organizations to monitor the Act. These are the Central Social Welfare Board, the Indian Council for Child Welfare, the Association for Consumers Action on Safely and Health, and the Breast-feeding Promotion Network of India (BPNI).

The Convention of the Rights of the Child, led to the formulation of the Innocent Declaration where 32 governments and ten UN agencies participated. The Innocent Declaration set four national targets to achieve by 1995:

12. To appoint a national level coordinator and establish a multisectoral national committee with representatives from the government, non-government organizations and the health profession.
13. To ensure that the health care institutions concerned with maternity services practice the ten steps to successful breast-feeding set out in the WHO/UNICEF statement.
14. To effect changes in marketing breast milk substitutes.
15. Enact legislation to protect the rights of working women to breast-feed their child.

Recognizing hospital deliveries of children as a major reason for decline in traditional breast-feeding patterns, the Innocent

Declaration requires every facility providing maternity services and care for newborn infants to follow the '10 Steps to Successful Breast-feeding".

30. Have a written breast-feeding policy that is routinely communicated to all the health care staff.
31. Train all health care staff in skills necessary to implement this policy.
32. Inform all pregnant women about the benefits and management of breast-feeding.
33. Help mother initiate breast-feeding within half an hour of birth.
34. Show mothers how to breast-feed and how to maintain lactation even if they should be separated from their infants.
35. Give newborn infants no food or drink other than breast milk, unless medically indicated.
36. Practice rooming-in that is allow mothers and infants to remain together 24 hours a day.
37. Encourage breast-feeding on demand.
38. Give no artificial teats/pacifiers to breast-fed infants.
39. Foster the establishment of breast-feeding support groups and refer mothers to them on discharge from hospital/clinic.

The Innocent Declaration led to the World Summit for Children, which finally led to the formation of the World Alliance for the Breast-feeding Action (WABA), a consortium of major international NGOs in 1991.

One important aspect of actually moving towards the targets set by the Innocent Declaration is the Baby Friendly Hospital Initiative (BFHI) launched in 1992. India has been one of the first supporters of the BFHI. Even before the BFHI came into India, the country's first Human Milk Bank had been established, in the mid-eighties, in the Lokmanya Tilak Hospital, Mumbai. However, this is an isolated example and cannot be interpreted as a response of hospitals to promote breast-feeding. India, in its National Program of Action for Children, set itself the goal to ensure that at least 1000 hospitals became 'Baby Friendly', by 1995. One-third of this target was achieved.

In 1993, a National Task Force for the BFHI was formed with representatives from voluntary and professional bodies. Under this project a training manual and video was produced. This global internal and external assessment criteria were adapted to the Indian context. In the first phase, the activity spanned five cities, and core trainers and assessors were created. In the first eighteen months, eighteen hospitals were classified officially as being BFHI, and the campaign spread to other areas. Taking into consideration the size and diversity of the country, the National Task Force moved to decentralize the campaign. During 1993 and 1994 coalitions were formed with the State Governments, professionals and the NGOs in fourteen states and state-level task forces were set up to look into training, dissemination of materials/information and to bring about change. This resulted in the increase of Baby Friendly Hospitals from 103 at the start of 1995 to a current number of 376. The UNICEF 1995 Progress Report on BFHI highlights the following:

— Substantial support of the medical professional establishment (the Indian Medical Association even offers a correspondence lactation course to its members).

— Decentralization of operations to reach out to hospital also and community health personnel.

— To target hospitals/maternity facilities so as to cover medical institutions with maternity services having over 1000 births per year.

— The State Governments of Tamil Nadu and Orissa have instructed all hospitals/maternity facilities within the two states to incorporate the BFHI program into their services.

The BPNI was formed in December, 1991. The network was an outcome of a ten-day workshop, 'Recent Advances in Human Lactation and Breast-feeding Management', jointly organized by the Indian Academy of Pediatrics (IAP), Federation of Obstetrics and Gynecological Societies of India (FOGSI) and Association for Consumer Action on Safety and Health (ACASH). The BPNI has a membership of 653 spread over 150 cities in India. It has 20 state and 100 city coordinators. It is primarily involved in:

— Training of medical personnel;

— Organizing World Breast-feeding Week (WBW) with WABA;
— Publications;
— Training materials;
— Research;
— Video production;
— Monitoring the implementation of the Infant Milk Substitutes, Feeding Bottles and Infant Foods Act (1992); and
— Introduction of topics related to breast-feeding in medical schools related professional training.

The BPNI is also involved with the National Task Force of' the BFHI. It trains personnel and monitors the BFHI. The Maharashtra Branch of the BPNI recognized the need to tie up with the state health machinery, to be able to make headway in government run health infrastructure, which forms a large chunk of services. Out of this need, emerged the Maharashtra Breast-feeding Promotion Initiative (MBPI), in May 1994. Its terms of reference are formulation, support and monitoring of groups for the three components of training, BFHI assessment and the monitoring of the Act.

As a result of the government resolution passed in April 1995, a committee comprising representatives from government departments and professional bodies has been constituted under the chairpersonship of the Director General, Health Services. This is a welcome initiative, for it offers an opportunity to several bodies in the state to contribute to the promotion of breast-feeding, like the BPNI, Directorate of Medical Education and Research, Indian Medical Association (IMA), Indian Academy of Pediatrics (IAP), FOGSI, National Neonatal Forum, Trained Nurses Association of India (TNAI), Indian Association of Preventive and Social Medicine, Association of Consumer's Action on Safety and Health and the NICEF.

Articles 42, 47, 39, and 15(3) in the Constitution of India provide the basic framework for legislation concerning maternity. They place emphasis on the provision of maternity relief at the workplace; state responsibility for nutrition and improvement of public health and ensure that the health and strength of men and women workers as well as children as a whole are not exploited; and that children are given opportunities and facilities to develop into healthy citizens with freedom and dignity.

The Factories Act, 1948; the Mines Act, 1950; the Plantations Act, 1951; the Bidi and Cigar Workers Act, 1966; the Contract Labor Act, 1970; the Inter-state Migrant Workers Act, 1980 - all provide for the setting up of creches at the workplace. A creche at the workplace helps the working mother to breast-feed the baby. The present legislations are linked to the number of working women in a given establishment. Instead, the criteria should be the number of eligible infants and children of all employees.

The two main Acts dealing with maternity benefits are the Employees State Insurance Act, 1948, and the Maternity Benefit Act, 1961. There have been several amendments to these Acts since they came into force. Maternity leave of 12 weeks is permitted. The mother can distribute this before/after delivery as per her convenience. In some states like Punjab and Haryana, 24 weeks of maternity leave is permitted. The difficulty with these maternity benefits is that they apply only to the organized sector, while the vast majority of women in the unorganized sectors cannot avail of them.

It is well-known that legislation is supportive to public awareness and education. By itself it can achieve little. The role of the Government in the campaign has been mainly by way of enacting favorable legislations. Besides this, it has program of supplementary feeding for pregnant and lactating mothers. It has Generally been supportive of voluntary organizations, though financial support has been minimal.

Medical education on infant feeding dealt in minute detail on the preparation of formula feeds for different acre groups of infants. Breast-feeding was never dealt with. It was perhaps taken for granted. Thus, professionals were trained to advise on bottle-feeding. Further, it was no secret that the infant milk industry used health professionals to promote their products. In this context, it is interesting to note that the movement for promotion of breast-feeding in India is lead by pediatrician today. Since 1980, the IAP has been moving towards independence from the baby food industry. Around this period, Nestle, the third largest producer of substitute breast milk products had offered a donation to an IAP official. The Academy unanimously refused the offer as they saw a conflict of interest. The Academy's workshops on consumer protection and lactation management are held without aid from the baby food industry. The pediatric quiz for undergraduate students is also now conducted by the Academy in place of Nestle and Wipro, the companies that had been doing it for several years.

In 1994, a brand leader among, multinational formula companies in India offered to pay all the expenses of the Academy's 8th Asian Congress of Pediatrics (estimated to be Rs. 10-15 million). The offer was turned down. The IAP being a medical professional body, has been responsible for roping in several other medical professional bodies like IMA, FOGSI, TNAI, and others. The IMA, with a membership of 1,00,000, has decided not to take any support from the baby food industry.

Social Work in Family Planning

Contraceptive behavior has been explained amply in terms of socio-economic characteristics at the individual as well as social level. But the propagation of contraception being a major responsibility of Governments in developing countries, the strength of the program has always been viewed as an important determinant of contraceptive behavior in a population. In fact, it has been argued that a good quality supply of the services can engineer its own demand for contraception.

In India, during 1950 and 60s, the family planning program was carried out independently through family planning clinics, initially as a clinic-based program followed by the extension approach. Integration of health, family planing and maternal and child health services was aimed at during the Fourth Five Year Plan. It was thought that instead of setting up an independent infrastructure for family planning services, it would be wiser to use the already existing infrastructure for providing health services. Another argument in favor of such an, integration was that it would lend credibility to the family planning program. The health personnel providing the welfare services would have better access and rapport with the community and hence would be in an advantageous position to propagate contraception. Almost thirty years have elapsed since the integration but we still do not have enough evidence to understand whether this well-intentioned strategy of integrating family planning services with MCH services has had beneficial implications in terms of synergising the two programs.

A number of experimental studies have been conducted to examine the effectiveness of the integration of health and family planning services. In India, studies such as the one conducted in Narangwal in Punjab and the other in Jamkhed in Maharashtra, have shown that such integration can lead to a considerable reduction in the levels of fertility and mortality.

However, such studies are rarely flawless; whether randomization is used in the selection of the treatment and the control areas and the extent to which matching is employed while making the comparison (between the outputs of treatment and control areas), it can have considerable influence on the results of the evaluation. Doubts have also been raised about the replicability of such studies. Survey-based researches have also been attempted to understand the linkages between health and family planning programs. This is generally attempted by comparing fertility and contraceptive practice between women who utilize health services and those who do not. The integration of family planning with health services, especially maternal and child hearth services, was found to have a positive influence on the family planning program in India

Arguments have been put forth to support the benefits of integrated programs for health and family planning. Such arguments are mainly based on the presumption that attitude towards and practice of family planning would improve if family planning were integrated with health services. Such a hypothesis originates from the theoretical supposition that MCH can bring about a reduction in infant and child mortality which will lead to increased contraceptive practice because of attitude changes associated with the expectation that more children would survive.

It has also been suggested that family planning and maternal health care strengthen one another in reducing maternal morbidity and mortality and hence should co-exist. There are, however, caveats in the integration of family planning with health services. Family planning should be a people's program. Integration means its being dominated by health personnel. Health professionals may have the credibility to run the program but may lack the ability to make it a people's program. Again the integration might lead to a narrowing down of the focus of family planning. It might get geared to only those requiring MCH services and neglect those not in need of such services.

It is true that any undue emphasis on one program will be detrimental to the other. It has been pointed out, in the context of the Indian program, that the integration, if anything, has resulted in the deterioration of MCH services due to the overemphasis on achieving family planning targets, particularly sterilization targets It would be of interest therefore to understand whether and to what extent the integration of family planning services with MCH might have led to better contraceptive behavior in the country.

Provision of MCH services is expected to serve as an initial step in furthering the contact beneficiaries and program personnel, which might facilitate the extent of motivation towards the use of contraception. Understanding this aspect assumes greater significance in view of the fact that there has been a gradual but sustained emphasis on reproductive health care and the Child Survival and Safe Motherhood (CSSM) program which was introduced in the country since 1992. If it were true that the integration did promote family planning without hampering the MCH program, it would be all the more prudent to make the integration stronger and more fruitful. Otherwise, there is a possibility that such an, integration could actually result in lowering the potentiality of both these crucial programs. The 1992-93 National Family Health Survey provides an opportunity to examine the possible linkages between the two programs.

The survey interviewed a total of 89,777 ever-married women in the age group of 1349 from 25 states covering more than 99 per cent of India's population. The data collection was carried out in three phases during April 1992 and September 1993. The survey was based on a systematic, multistage, stratified sample design. The major topics covered in the NFHS include fertility, marriage pattern, family size preferences, the level of unwanted fertility, knowledge and practice of family planning, the potential demand for contraception, utilization of antenatal services, breast-feeding and food supplementation services, child health and nutrition, vaccination, and infant and child mortality.

Over the years, the family planning (FP) programme is showing varying impacts on fertility across regions and population groups in India. The success of FP is becoming increasingly a regional phenomenon. The process of fertility decline in India is being negated by the low effect of FP among weaker sections, most of whom live under conditions of poverty. The success stories of FP in Kerala and Tamil Nadu highlight that the success of FP is largely due to its diffusion, which has been greatly facilitated by regional social factors. For the last few decades, scores of studies have stressed that wide differences exist in FP adoption across religions and caste groups and the variations always have been markedly higher among low castes and Muslims (weaker sections).

The results of India's first-ever National Family Health Survey (NFHS), conducted during 1992-93, indicate that the current use of contraception in the country is relatively lower among SCs, STs, and Muslims. The NFHS also reveals that the mean number of children born and the ideal family size desired are comparatively higher among them. It is important to note that the weaker section is mainly a configuration of BCs, SCs, STs and Muslim communities who, together, comprise nearly two-thirds of the country's population.

Low acceptance of contraception among these communities would certainly have a significant impact on the prospects of FP performance and on the process of fertility decline too. Therefore, in the context of strengthening efforts towards accelerating the process of fertility decline among the Vulnerable groups for achieving the national demographic goals, evaluation of FP practice's among these communities has assumed greater importance in recent years. While several factors could have contributed to the low acceptance of contraception among weaker sections, our aim, in this exercise, is to analyse the Process of FP diffusion among BCs in relation to the influence of caste and changing social conditions.

Two factors have been very frequently mentioned in the context of low acceptance of FP among weaker sections, viz.,

(a) the existence of strong apprehensions in these communities that the adoption of FP methods will lead to smaller family size which, in turn, may adversely affect their social and economic security in life, particularly during illness and old age, and it may also lead to serious health problems; and

(b) adoption of uniform FP strategies, notwithstanding differences in socioeconomic conditions across the population groups in the country.

Adoption of FP, being voluntary in India, it is necessary that significant changes must occur in the fertility attitudes of the people towards adoption of the small family norm, and 'social acceptance of FP methods for producing greater results in FP. It is argued that this approach has been lacking in FP strategies, especially towards weaker sections, which has resulted in lower acceptance among them. Interestingly, even in regions Or among populations where FP has achieved a great success, it was preceded by processes Of social adoption of the small family norm, attitudinal changes and popular acceptance of FP.

There are a number of ways in which popular acceptance of FP can occur:

(1) effective delivery of FP services, intensive FP campaign through mass media, organized movements about FP adoption, and intensification of FP campaign as has been done during the Emergency in India, and

(2) increased inputs in FP, as in the case of India Population Project districts and Matalab of Bangladesh, etc.

The diffusion in FP can also occur spontaneously because of improvement in living conditions which, in turn, may lead to changes in perception about large family size. In addition, social and cultural changes taking place within the community too contribute to such diffusions. It would, however be unwise to attribute the diffusion of FP to any one factor, especially when several factors operate simultaneously in the community. Nevertheless, the diffusion is operated mostly through social channels, as the population of the country consists of a large number of illiterates. This being the cast, FP information is conveyed to the population mostly through interpersonal communication, which is very effective when taking, decisions about FP adoption.

The social structure wig have greater influence on the spread of FP adoption, because, such changes occur in the social system. While homogeneous groups facilitate, free and easy flow of information about FP, heterogeneous groups, segregated by social norms, statuses and hierarchy, inhibit free flow of communication about FP adoption and hamper the process of FP diffusion.

Caste is a major actor in the social system, particularly in rural communities, its influences are strong and manifold on the diffusion process of FP.

First, it serves as a crucial channel for communicating FP messages and initiating changes in fertility attitudes.

Secondly, the FP campaigns effect dissemination in different ways across caste groups according to their socio-economic and cultural status in the community, and their position in the hierarchy can facilitate and expedite, or impede the process of FP diffusion.

Thirdly, caste differentiation's can lead to disparities in accessibility, utilization and in the quality of health and FP services in the community, which, in turn, can hamper the process of FP diffusion.

Finally, when the community is predominated by same caste members or homogeneous groups, it facilitates the process of social acceptance of the small family norm and also accelerates the diffusion of FP.

It is widely recognized that the high castes have high socioeconomic status and greater cultural adaptability to innovations and interventions, which, in turn, quickly induce changes in their fertility attitudes during the FP campaign. The high caste members are mostly literate, economically better-off, have better access to health, transport and communication facilities, and have greater exposure to the outside world. Hence, adaptation of the small family norm and diffusion of FP would occur much earlier, and at a faster rate among them.

In contrast, the inherent socio-economic conditions among low castes make them less susceptible to interventions and innovations. They are largely illiterate, economically weak, highly concentrated in rural areas, deprived of opportunities to outside exposure, have less access to health and communication facilities, and their fertility attitudes are strongly influenced by superstition and cultural factors. Therefore, the process of FP diffusion would be relatively slower in taking root among them.

In recent years, health and family welfare services have expanded significantly, particularly in rural areas, with the establishment of a larger number of primary health centres, and the intensification of Maternal and Child Health (MCH) services. This apart, several developmental and welfare programmes have been launched, 'by both government and voluntary agencies, for improving the socio-economic conditions of the weaker sections, during the last few years.

These programmes relate mainly to providing such basic needs as supply of drinking water, providing housing and sanitation facilities, supply of essential commodities at subsidized rates, expansion of primary and adult education, creation of employment opportunities, agricultural and animal husbandry development, land reforms and a host of other financial assistance schemes.

It should be noted that effective delivery of FP and other welfare programmes to the weaker sections can be constrained by certain organizational and peripheral problems like lack of adequate communication and transport facilities, and poor coverage of benefits due to their high participation in the labours-force, interior location of houses, etc.

It is important to note here that rapid societal changes are occurring simultaneously in the population due to a variety of reasons, such as greater opportunities for social exposure and inter-community relations, rise in income levels as a consequence of diversification of economic activities, expansion of communication facilities and mass media, etc. Consequently, these factors take different forms in initiating changes in fertility attitudes and FP adoption among weaker sections.

Mental Health Social Work

The past fifty years has seen the emergence of a vast range of therapies and a therapeutic culture in which the public now accepts that troubled and traumatised people should receive professional help. This has increased the demand for treatment for psychological problems and contributed to the rapid growth of private clinics and therapies. As a result the notion of universality in mental health services is becoming meaningless. The development of a two-tier system means that the better-off have an element of choice, while poorer people have to accept what is offered.

Although governments have given health and social services a clear remit to promote mental health for all and to reduce the discrimination experienced by people with mental health problems the underlying thinking is very confused. In fact the 'socially inclusive' strategy seems to imply that the 'mentally ill' are in some way responsible for their problems! Politicians have totally distorted the concept of social exclusion, which was originally associated with poverty and inequality. They assume that the 'mentally ill' are people who live apart from the rest of society, which is a myth, and who need to be helped to participate in community life. This way of thinking avoids any philosophical discussion of the place of 'the outsider' in society and overlooks the possibility that 'the outsider' may be a positive identity.

The socially inclusive strategy is more about getting the mentally ill into paid work than about tackling their very real problems of poverty, deprivation and stigma. Although strategies are emerging which address inequalities caused by gender and race little can be achieved if more fundamental inequalities caused by class are overlooked. It is alarming that much of the publicity surrounding the government thinking on mental health services seems to be working to increase the stigma attached to mental illness.

The most common reaction when anyone dares to admit to suffering from a mental illness, particularly manic depression or, worst of all schizophrenia, is fear. This attitude not only adversely affects the sufferer's own perception of themselves but also has very real practical effects on their lives and their employment prospects.

In order to get any worthwhile job they have to lie about their medical history, which means living in perpetual fear of discovery, and they are unable to have a normal relationship with colleagues because they are continually hiding what comes to seem a shameful secret. It is not uncommon, too, for them to feel that they have brought shame on their family and they cannot even tell their closest friends. Surely it is the stigma of mental illness that is a real barrier to 'social inclusion'. Social workers certainly have an uphill task if they are to tackle this.

In the past people with mental health problems were always considered a low priority for social work help. The suffering of mentally ill people was largely discounted by the policy-makers within social services departments. Social workers are now finding a role for themselves in community mental health teams (CMHT) and developing their skills using ideas from counselling and therapy but there is a serious risk that these social workers could lose their core professional identity.

It is important that social workers continue to provide an alternative to the bio-medical approach which puts the emphasis on controlling symptoms with medication and helping people to accept the status quo. Social work believes the social model is essential in this work and strives to empower clients and raise awareness of the social and psychological causes of problems.

A key philosophical question for social workers is whether help is offered according to clients' own definition of need or whether the over-riding aim is the re-adjustment of the client towards conventional norms of behaviour. There is also the problem of the vagueness of the concept of 'need' in mental health work and clients often being unable to express needs in a clear and straightforward way.

Many people with mental health problems are more accustomed to concealing than revealing their problems. Now that the care management model underpins service delivery social workers have to be very creative in finding ways of bringing together the structured, rational world of care management and the often messy, chaotic lives of clients and their families. The social worker who reaches out to the mentally ill person and maintains an ongoing relationship can do a great deal to assist that person's recovery. It is the consistency of caring, the human relationship, and the sense of a meeting between equals that is important in this work. A client going through a breakdown is likely to have problems functioning in the home, at work, in the community and the social worker may be expected to meet a wide range of needs until the client recovers.

In the world of increasingly bureaucratised and depersonalised statutory services the social worker often provides the human face of the organisation. In addition, the social worker seeks out resources and groups in the community where the client may be able to find ongoing support.

Mental health social work has been struggling ever since the creation of social services departments to establish itself as a specialist area of social work with a clear professional identity. The emergence of the approved social worker helped to establish a role but it now looks as though even this could be taken away. The future for mental health social workers in community teams still looks rather uncertain.

The low status of the social worker is not the fault of social workers but those responsible for creating a selfish society which ignores the plight of the weakest and most vulnerable. Mental health social workers carry enormous responsibilities and do important preventive work. Re- establishing mental health social work as a radical activity is essential if it is to survive with some degree of professionalism and independence.

Social Work and Eduation

International Association of Schools of Social work (IASSW) is a global network of schools of social work and educators at tertiary level that identifies and encourages quality education, training and research for the theory and practice of social work, the administration of social services and the formulation of social policies for social work. IASSW operates as an NGO (non-governmental organisation) in the five regions of Africa, Asia and the Pacific, Europe, Latin America and North America. IASSW Mission is

1. To develop and promote world wide excellence in social work education, research and scholarship in order to enhance human well being.
2. To create and maintain a dynamic community of social work educators and their programs.
3. To support and facilitate participation in mutual exchanges of information and expertise.
4. To represent social work education at the international level. In fulfilling its mission, members adhere to all United Nations Declarations and Conventions on human rights and recognise that respect for the inalienable rights of the individual is the foundation of freedom, justice and peace. Additionally IASSW fosters cooperation, collegiality and interdependence among

members and with others, engages in the pursuit of social justice and social development.

References

Agnew, Elizabeth N. (2004). *From Charity to Social Work: Mary E. Richmond and the Creation of an American Profession*. Urbana, IL: University of Illinois Press.

Richardson, Virginia E. and Amanda Smith Barusch (2006). *Gerontological Practice for the Twenty-First Ccentury: A Social Work Perspective*. New York, NY: Columbia University Press.

Thomas, K. W. and Velthouse, B. A. (1990) Cognitive Elements of Empowerment: An 'Interpretive' Model of Intrinsic Task Motivation. *Academy of Management Review*, Vol 15, No. 4, 666-681.

Wilkinson, A. 1998. *Empowerment: theory and practice. Personnel Review*. [online]. Vol. 27, No. 1, 40-56. Available from: Emerald on the World Wide Web.

2

Empowerment in Practice

Empowerment—that is, enhancing an individual's or group's capacity to make choices and transform those choices into desired actions and outcomes—is an increasingly familiar term within the World Bank and many other development agencies.

First recognised by the Bank in its World Development Report 2000/2001 as one of the three pillars of poverty reduction, empowerment is now found in the documentation of over 1,800 World Bank-aided projects, and it is the subject of debate and analytic work within the development community. Despite growing interest and increased investments in empowerment, the development of instruments and indicators with which to monitor and evaluate empowerment processes and outcomes is still at an early stage.

Measuring Empowerment

If a person or group is empowered, they possess the capacity to make *effective* choices; that is, to translate their choices into desired actions and outcomes. In a five-country study on measuring empowerment currently overseen by the World Bank's empowerment team, it is assumed that degrees of empowerment can be measured. This capacity to make an effective choice is primarily influenced by two sets of factors: agency and opportunity structure. Agency is defined as an actor's ability to make meaningful choices; that is, the actor is able to envisage options and make a choice. Opportunity structure is defined as the formal and informal contexts within which actors operate. Working together, these factors give rise to different degrees of empowerment.

Agency and opportunity structure are hypothesised to associate with the degree of empowerment a person or group experiences. Degrees of empowerment (DOE) can be measured by assessing (1) whether a person has the opportunity to make a choice, (2) whether a person actually uses the opportunity to choose, and (3) once the choice is made, whether it brings the desired outcome.

While we currently have much anecdotal and case study evidence to suggest an instrumental purpose in empowering people, robust data demonstrating a clear association between empowerment and development outcomes are hard to find. There are plenty of data available on the association between intermediary indicators of empowerment—agency and opportunity structure—and development outcomes. However, because of a paucity of data on direct indicators of empowerment, the relationship between empowerment and development outcomes remains a hypothesis.

Agency

How can agency—the capacity to make meaningful choice—be measured? In the five-country study, and increasingly in other project monitoring systems, *asset endowments* are used as indicators of agency. These assets can be psychological, informational, organisational, material, social, financial, or human. Some assets are easier to measure than others. For example, it is easier to quantify human assets than psychological assets or social assets.

Understanding the complex interaction among assets also presents challenges. The endowment of a single asset, such as ownership of land, can affect a person's ability to make meaningful choices. In addition, an actor's or group's command over one asset can affect the endowment of another asset. In this case, all three assets contribute to an actor's capacity to make meaningful choices. Therefore, data have to be gathered on a range of assets, and analysis can, if relevant, test for the effects of one asset on another as well as for their effects on empowerment outcomes.

Opportunity Structure

As demonstrated by the earlier examples from India and Benin, an actor's opportunity structure is shaped by the presence and operation of formal and informal institutions, or rules of the game. These include the laws, regulatory frameworks, and norms governing people's behaviour. The presence and operation of the formal and informal laws, regulations, norms, and customs determine whether individuals and groups have access to assets, and whether these people can use the assets to achieve desired outcomes.

Measuring opportunity structure involves analysing the presence and the operation of formal and informal institutions. Collecting and analysing data may require a mixed-methods approach. For example, information on the presence of particular legislation can be drawn from secondary sources, but data on the actual operation of that formal institution within a particular community would likely require interviews with a range of respondents. Gathering data on the presence and operation of informal institutions may require a similar dual approach. It may also be important to take preliminary results back to key stakeholders for verification and discussion of anomalies or options for responding to undesirable findings.

Degrees of Empowerment

Measurement of assets and institutions provides intermediary indicators of empowerment. Direct measures of empowerment can be made by assessing:

1. Whether an opportunity to make a choice exists.
2. Whether a person actually uses the opportunity to choose.
3. Whether the choice resulted in the desired result.

To illustrate, if a team were trying to assess the degree of political empowerment of women, it would need to gather information on (1) whether opportunities for political participation exist, such as whether elections are held, and, if so, (2) whether women attempt to vote; and (3) whether they actually vote. For several reasons, including the geographic, social, or economic positioning of a person or group, the opportunity to make a desired choice may not exist.

Where Empowerment Takes Place—Domains and Levels

Using agency and opportunity structure to frame analysis of

empowerment is helpful, but leads to two further questions. First, does a person's capacity to make effective choices vary according to *what* he or she is doing? Second, does empowerment vary according to the *level* at which a person is acting?

An Indian woman will experience a form of empowerment when she is trying to exercise choice over domestic resources within the household different from that which she will experience when in a bank trying to access a loan. Her experiences will also differ according to whether she is trying to operate in her village, at a market or office located at a distance from her village, or in a capital city. These added complexities in the measurement of empowerment are dealt with by conceptualising three different domains and three different levels of actors' lives.

This conceptualisation is important to an analytic framework that has to span the multiple political, social, and economic conditions found in different countries. As the following discussion illustrates, the three domains and levels apply in each country.

Domains

The five-country study identifies three domains:

— State, in which a person is a civic actor.

— Market, in which a person is an economic actor.

— Society, in which a person is a social actor.

The three domains are further divided into eight sub-domains:

— The domain of state is divided into the sub-domains of justice, politics, and service delivery.

— The domain of market is divided into the sub-domains of credit, labour, and goods (for both production and consumption).

— The domain of society is divided into the sub-domains of family and community. These should be treated as opportunities to explore relations within the household and within the community. In certain contexts it may be necessary to refine or add to these sub-domains.

In each of these sub-domains, the individual actor experiences a certain degree of empowerment. This is likely to vary between people or groups.

In the state domain, citizens may experience very different degrees of empowerment in terms of accessing justice, participating in politics, or accessing social services. In India, a well educated, high-caste man with good social connections would experience a higher degree of empowerment in all three sub-domains than his low-caste, illiterate counterpart.

In the market domain, one person or group may be able to access credit yet have no labour opportunities or purchasing power. However, another group or person may have different experiences.

In the domain of society, a son in an Indian household is likely to experience a higher degree of empowerment than a daughter, yet, in her community, a high-caste daughter would experience a higher degree of empowerment than the daughter of a low-caste family.

While no prior assumption can be made about how empowerment in any one domain or sub-domain relates to empowerment in some other domain or sub-domain, the degree of empowerment in one sub-domain may well correlate with a similar degree of empowerment in another domain.

Levels

People experience domains and sub-domains at different levels—macro, intermediary, and local. For ease of analysis, *a level* is defined as an administrative boundary. These levels are common in most countries. In India, where the vast size of a country means that states are extremely important administrative units, the macro level could correspond to the state, the intermediary to the district, and the local to the village. In India, it may also be necessary to add a supra-macro, federal level.

Another feature generalisable across countries is the distance of administrative boundaries from the individual or group.

— The local level will comprise the immediate vicinity of a person's everyday life. This is likely to be the level of an area contiguous with their residence.

— The intermediary level will comprise a vicinity which is familiar but which is not encroached upon on an everyday basis. This is likely to be the level between the residential and national level.

— The macro level will comprise a vicinity which is the furthest away from the individual. This is likely to be the national level.

Empowerment can be assessed at different domains of a person's life and at different levels. Each domain can be divided into sub-domains, which will indicate where and in what areas of their lives actors are empowered. At the intersection of the domains and levels, people can experience different degrees of empowerment, addressing the issues of whether and to what extent a person is empowered. Two clusters of interdependent factors associate with the different degrees of empowerment an individual or group experiences—the agency of the actor and the opportunity structure within which that actor operates.

ME FRAMEWORK—APPLICATIONS

The ME framework provides an analytic structure that can be used to (1) monitor change and evaluate the impact of a specific project that has empowerment as one of its goals, (2) conduct in-depth research, (3) monitor national-level concerns, and (4) track relative changes in empowerment among different countries. The objective and context of each activity will determine which aspects of the framework to use and how to collect and analyse data.

An in-depth research exercise could seek to understand whether, how, and to what extent marginalised people, such as Indian women, can be empowered. To develop policy and practice recommendations, such research would need to focus on all sub-domains and levels identified by the analytic framework.

A national-level monitoring exercise can use the ME framework to identify key indicators in each domain and undertake an analysis of empowerment at different levels.

Finally, using the ME framework concepts of domains and levels allows a comparative assessment of empowerment across countries. While some argue that inter-country comparisons are pointless, others indicate that information of this kind can encourage governments to improve performance. In fact, this has already happened as a result of the international governance reviews and databases now available to compare performance in governance across countries.

Two points are important in relation to these various applications. The first concerns the need for context-specific data collection and analysis. The second relates to conceptual differences regarding terms used in data collection and analysis. First, as indicated above, the analytic framework is flexible in that it identifies what is important to measure, but it does not prescribe the depth of substantive coverage of data collection or analysis for any particular use. However, indicators, variables, and their values must be country and context-specific. Therefore, for the five countries in which the study was undertaken, each country team decided for themselves the levels to examine, the indicators to use for measurement, and the values placed on variables. Some analysts may be uncomfortable with this flexibility, but the scope and scale of information gathered, along with prior information on the context, will help analysts hypothesise likely associations and causal relations for testing.

The second point is that the level about which information is gathered, the level at which it is gathered and the level of pooling of information for analysis are conceptually and practically distinct. Levels about which data are collected refer to administrative boundaries, such as a woman's empowerment in a household, a community, or a district headquarters. This is different from the level at which data collection is undertaken. Further, both levels about and levels of data collection are distinct from pooling, or levels at which data are analysed. The information and data resulting from that survey are usually pooled and analysed at an intermediary or national level—such as in the case of an LSMS or national poverty monitoring exercise.

Examples of Application in Interventions

Feedback from project teams indicates that the application of the framework for structuring analysis and developing empowerment indicators is a manageable task. Lead researchers for each case study were either involved in the development of the framework or briefed on its content by the coordinating team.

(i) *Applying the Framework in Ethiopia: The Women's Development Initiatives Project (WDIP)*

The ME framework structured the design of the Women's

Development Initiatives Project's (WDIP's) impact evaluation. The evaluation assesses the empowerment status of Ethiopian women in both rural and urban areas in general, and then examines whether enhancements in their empowerment associate with their participation in WDIP. The project aims to strengthen women's self-help groups as a mechanism to increase their economic, social, and political opportunities.

WDIP is a community-driven development project that seeks to enhance women's empowerment and participation in development interventions by mobilising women at the grassroots level and capitalising on their potential to support development processes. It does so by facilitating the formation of self-help groups, strengthening existing grassroots groups, and enhancing women's capacity to act collectively, thereby increasing the social and economic welfare of their households.

The Government of Ethiopia, recognising the disadvantaged position of women, has implemented a number of policies, laws, and initiatives to promote women's empowerment, such as removing discriminatory laws from the constitution. With the announcement of the National Policy on Women in 1993 and promulgation of the new constitution in 1995, the government highlighted its commitment to the equal development of women. However, these policies and laws are often weakly enforced. The underlying rationale for launching the project is that women remain among some of the poorest and most severely disadvantaged of citizens. WDIP aims to redress gender imbalances in development opportunity by investing in women's skills, productivity, and organisational capacity. The project components include (1) a demand-driven fund that finances women's group activities, such as handicraft production, the rearing of animals and poultry, and the organisation of a day-care centre; (2) capacity building and training for women's groups and other project stakeholders on organisation, facilitation, project design, appraisal, and monitoring and evaluation; and (3) information, education, and communication activities that enhance gender awareness.

Measuring Empowerment in WDIP

This exercise has two objectives: (1) to examine the general empowerment status of poor women in Ethiopia, and (2) to assess the impact WDIP may have on women's empowerment. Communities are selected from the Amhara and Addis Ababa regions. Results from this qualitative enquiry were used to develop testable hypotheses and indicators, which then framed a quantitative survey. Data collected using a household survey instrument are currently under analysis.

Qualitative data were collected in communities where WDIP is present from both beneficiaries and non-beneficiaries. During the quantitative stage as well, data were collected for both the treatment and a control group.

The qualitative and quantitative instruments gather data on women's assets, their opportunity structure, and degrees of empowerment in all three domains. Asset and degree of empowerment indicators mainly correspond to the local and intermediary level. Opportunity structure indicators also encompass the macro level.

This includes both how women are treated within the national judicial system and by the laws upheld in the traditional courts still operating in the country. Assets that may help women both increase their representation in the district councils and get a fair treatment in the juridical system include previous participation in associations or political parties as well as their level of education and self-confidence and the extent of their awareness of their rights. Opportunity structure indicators refer to formal rules of the game such as the existence of laws that ensure women equal treatment within the judicial system and grant them representation in community groups and councils. With regard to informal rules, indicators gauge the extent to which formal legislature may contradict or be in tension with traditional practices, making (a) women less likely to obtain justice than men, and/or (b) less able to engage in political matters/public life.

In the market domain/labour sub-domain, one of the degrees of empowerment indicators is the extent to which women are able to choose their type of employment. Asset indicators capture women's education and income levels, their possession of job-specific skills, and the extent to which they have access to different sources of information. Opportunity structure indicators capture the distance to the nearest market.

WDIP's impact evaluation also establishes a series of empowerment indicators for the society domain/family sub-domain, such as the percentage of women who have decision-making power equal to that of their husbands over the number and spacing of children, the use of contraceptives, and conjugal relations (family sub-domain). The qualitative enquiry led the study team to hypothesise that the extent to which women have a say in these matters associates with such assets as women's education, income, and self-confidence levels, their awareness of reproductive health issues, and their participation in women's groups.

(ii) Applying the Framework in Nepal: The Measuring Empowerment and Social Inclusion (MESI) Study

The Rural Water Supply and Sanitation Project I (RWSS project) was designed to build rural drinking water schemes and empower local citizens to undertake their construction and management. In addition, it had a clear objective of empowering women, and therefore provided fertile ground for measuring empowerment. The MESI study is the broadest and only longitudinal study among the five cases. It is also financed independently of the other four country cases.

The World Bank–funded RWSS project started in 1996. RWSS sought to promote decentralisation and increase the involvement of beneficiaries and the private sector in rural water supply and sanitation service delivery; inculcate a demand-driven approach in the drinking water and sanitation sector; enable communities to take lead roles in the identification, design, implementation, operation, and maintenance of their water supply and sanitation schemes; and develop adequate capacities in the government and non-government sectors to support community initiatives.

By far the largest component of the project is the construction of rural water supply and sanitation schemes in 900 rural communities. Normally, a sub-project takes 36 months and has three main phases: (1) predevelopment, involving feasibility studies and selection of support organisations; (2) development, in which the scheme is designed and the rural community is prepared to take ownership; and (3) implementation, involving construction, establishment of a community action plan, and transfer of ownership to the rural community.

(b) Measuring Empowerment in RWSS

RWSS communities are organised into "batches" that are brought into the project, following the three phases above. Subsequent batches incorporate the lessons learned from previous ones. Focusing on a sample of RWSS I Batch IV and Batch V schemes that will be completed during the first two years of RWSS II, MESI research seeks to assess whether and how the RWSS project has empowered communities in relation to government and NGO service providers, and asks whether women, Dalits, and Janajatis, as previously marginalised groups, have been empowered and experience greater social inclusion due to the RWSS intervention.

The MESI and the ME studies have collaborated on developing the overall framework for measurement, and both have used the same broad set of domains in operationalising the concepts of empowerment and social inclusion. The MESI study is designed as two phases of research on empowerment and inclusion, integrated into the RWSS project cycle. Each phase includes a qualitative and quantitative component. The first phase spanned nine months, and the second phase will span three years. The first phase was a self-contained research design that established the baseline of the longitudinal study that is the keystone of this research.

The state and society domains are covered, and the research concentrates on the intermediary and local levels. Data are collected on wide range of assets hypothesised to have a relationship with empowerment outcomes. Assets include standard measures such as literacy and land ownership, as well as group membership, participation in training, and knowledge of rights. Indicators of opportunity structure focus on the rules that govern social positioning, social interaction, physical mobility, violence, and economic security or vulnerability.

(iii) Applying the Framework in Honduras: The Community-Based Education Project (Proyecto Hondureño de Education Comunitaria, PROHECO)

PROHECO is an education decentralisation project that devolves decision-making authority over education matters to community-based school councils. In addition to assessing the impact PROHECO has had on education outcomes, a recent evaluation also sought to gauge the extent to which community members have become empowered in terms of the functions devolved to them by the project. The ME framework was used to establish hypotheses and empowerment indicators and to design instruments for data collection. General hypotheses tested include (1) whether the reform empowers school councils to have greater decision-making authority, and (2) whether it empowers different community members to participate in and have a voice in school council meetings.

Indicators were constructed to measure school councils' and community members' degrees of empowerment as well as their assets and opportunity structure. Both quantitative and qualitative instruments were designed for data collection.

PROHECO was launched in March 1999 with the objective of enhancing access to and quality of education as well as fostering community participation in school-related decision-making. Studies the Ministry of Education had carried out in 1997 showed that more than 14 percent of school-age children were not enrolled in schools; 85 percent of these children lived in rural areas. Building on the successful experiences in El Salvador and Guatemala, the Honduran government decided to establish new pre-schools and primary schools in remote rural villages, using a school-based management model (SBM). SBM is a type of education decentralisation reform, key to which is the creation of a school council responsible for making a series of decisions on administrative, personnel, pedagogical, and budget matters.

In Honduras, school councils comprise parents and other community members. They consist of two separate bodies: the general assembly and the board. Membership to the general assembly is granted automatically to all community members; only board membership requires a formal election process. PROHECO devolves the following functions and responsibilities to the school councils: building and maintaining the school; buying school supplies; overseeing the school's budget; and selecting, hiring, paying, monitoring and, if necessary, firing teachers.

Communities qualify for a PROHECO school if they meet the following criteria: (1) they are located in a rural area, (2) there are at least 25 pre-school and primary-school age children able to attend, (3) the nearest school is at least 3 km away, and (4) the village is located in an area that was affected by hurricane Mitch. Once communities are identified, a government employee visits them to inform them of the project and, if they agree to participate, helps them elect a school council. Training and support are crucial since communities are not familiar with carrying out the functions that the decentralisation reform devolves to them.

Measuring Empowerment in PROHECO

PROHECO's impact evaluation seeks to measure empowerment in the context of two power relationships that are potentially affected by the education reform. These are power relations (1) among different community members, and (2) between the school council and education authorities, including school staff. Related hypotheses state that the project empowers different community members to participate in and have a voice in school council meetings, irrespective of their gender, socio-economic status, or ethnicity.

Identifying these power relations and where they play out helped select the sub-domains and levels where empowerment is measured. It also helped determine the units and locus of data collection and analysis. The PROHECO evaluation addresses both the service delivery sub-domain and the household and community sub-domains.

Similar to WDIP and RWSS, the PROHECO evaluation uses a mixed-methods approach, applying institutional and household surveys at the quantitative stage as well as key informant and community interviews during the qualitative stage. The evaluation uses both a treatment and a control group, allowing for a comparison between schools managed by the community school council and those which are part of the traditional state-run system.

In terms of school council empowerment, the evaluation assesses whether the council is able to carry out its devolved functions. Indicators of degrees of empowerment therefore correspond to a council's capacity to build and maintain the school building, to buy school supplies, to oversee the budget, and to hire and fire teachers. Using the concepts of assets and opportunity structure, a series of factors that influence the council's capacity to assume its new tasks were determined. The opportunity structure for school council empowerment can be divided into (1) formal rules, such as the decrees and regulations that specify the details of the decentralisation reform, including the nature of the powers to be devolved to the school councils, and (2) a series of socio-political factors that shape how the reform is implemented in practice and whether it leads to the desired empowerment outcomes.

With regard to community empowerment, the evaluation seeks to assess whether and to what extent different family or community members are able to participate and have an effective voice in school council meetings and decision making. Of particular interest here is whether such attributes as gender, ethnicity, and socio-economic status deter or facilitate the participation or empowerment of specific groups. Degrees of empowerment indicators therefore relate to a person's involvement in school council activities.

Applying the ME Framework in Mexico

The ME analytic framework was recently used to establish draft empowerment indicators for the impact evaluation component of the Mexico Lifelong Learning Project, currently under preparation and recently appraised by the Bank. The project aims to provide secondary education to young adults (15 – 34 years old) who have dropped out of the formal education system but are demanding the conclusion of their lower secondary level education. In addition to improving students' literacy and numeracy thinking and problem-solving capacity, the modules offered aim to provide students with a series of skills and competencies to improve their quality of life and also strengthen their self-confidence. Participation in the project is therefore expected to improve a series of students' assets and, as a consequence, enhance their ability to make more informed choices and decisions, in other words, to become empowered.

The Mexico Lifelong Learning Project will give young adults who have dropped out of the formal school system the opportunity to complete the equivalent of a lower secondary education certificate. The project counterpart is the National Institute for Adult Education (INEA), which provides non-formal education to adults throughout the country. The pedagogical model INEA applies is known as "education for life and work." Its main characteristics are a competency-based curriculum, a modular design, and a recognition of individual potential and talent.

INEA offers literacy, primary and secondary education through a menu of entry points, including learning circles, peer facilitation and community learning centres. The community learning centres, in turn offer three different types of learning spaces: (1) "learning circles," where adults study, making use of printed materials and a facilitator, (2) IT rooms, where students learn to use computers and where they can study, making use of digital versions of their modules, and (3) a multimedia centre, where educational material is provided via television and videos.

In addition to providing students with modules in Spanish, math, and natural and social sciences, INEA also offer modules that aim to equip students with a diverse series of skills and competencies.

Applying the Framework in the Lifelong Learning Project

Monitoring and evaluation is one of the project's components. Impacts will be evaluated on a regular basis, using the following indicators: health, income, employment, continued education, and empowerment.

The project's impact evaluation system will define empowerment as enhancing a student's effective decision-making power. Education is crucial for empowerment because it improves students' assets, such as skills, confidence, and knowledge, thereby enabling them to make more informed and effective choices and decisions. However, while education is very important, it is not equal to empowerment. This in turn will be influenced by the opportunity structure in which they live and work.

In addition, investments in education, itself an asset, can have a positive impact on other assets as well as on empowerment outcomes. The core hypotheses framing the recurrent evaluations are therefore that (1) obtaining lower secondary education through participation in INEA's lifelong learning program will enhance students' assets, such as knowledge, skills, communication, and social capital, and (2) participation in INEA programs and the resulting asset improvements will empower students.

One modification made in this application of the ME framework is that the desire to choose and making a choice are treated as discrete degrees of empowerment. The degrees of empowerment therefore, for this project evaluation, become: (1) having awareness and information about a given situation, (2) having the will to act, (3) making a decision, and (4) achieving the desired outcome. Using "casting a vote in local elections" as an example indicator, the impact evaluation could ask (a) whether the respondent was aware of the last local elections, (b) whether she or he wanted to vote, (c) whether she or he then proceeded to vote, and (d) whether the cast vote was counted.

Participation in the Lifelong Learning Project intends to empower students in different domains of their lives. Each module offered to students has a specific purpose or intention, often reflecting the aim of providing students with the knowledge and skills to make more effective and informed decisions in different areas of their lives, in other words, to contribute to their empowerment. Modules about democracy and political participation are intended to empower students to become more active citizens. Modules that strengthen student self-esteem and inform them about sexual health issues empower them to insist on the use of condoms to prevent the infection with STDs. Modules in home mathematics skills have provided opportunities for the start of self-generated micro-enterprises. The choice of empowerment indicators reflects these intended outcomes.

Four groups of empowerment indicators have been identified. They fall into the following categories: (1) women's autonomous decision making within the household, (2) participation in public or political affairs, (3) taking action to improve one's work situation, and (4) making decisions to improve one's health.

Evaluating empowerment outcomes within different domains/ sub-domains allows the evaluation team to compare whether empowerment outcomes are the same for different domains, and to assess whether modules contribute to their intended outcomes.

The impact of the project on students will be evaluated on a biannual basis, with the first evaluation expected to be completed in 2005. The data collected during this first evaluation will serve as the baseline for future evaluations.

Applying the Framework within a National Survey

At the national level, empowerment has become embedded in the language of national policy frameworks for poverty reduction. A recent review of some 39 Poverty Reduction Strategy Papers (PRSPs) and Interim Poverty Reduction Strategy Papers (IPRSPs) (Thin), for example, reveals that almost half of this sample explicitly mentions empowerment in some shape or form. The scope of discussion of empowerment issues and strategies within these PRSPs, however, is quite narrow. The three predominant thematic areas of discussing empowerment, echoed in a recent PREM review are governance, gender, and community participation. Governance is discussed particularly in the context of decentralisation and service provision. Here, empowerment strategies focus on strengthening agency and "voice" through education, capacity building, and enhanced knowledge, while tackling "responsiveness" through public-sector reform and capacity building among service providers. Community participation is also widely addressed, emphasising participation in the project cycle linked to ownership and sustainability, with, in some cases, specific reference to natural resource management.

Furthermore, although empowerment appears as an objective in many PRSPs, recent efforts to assess the extent to which these commitments have been achieved demonstrate the paucity of data available for such evaluations. The absence of instruments and reliable data for monitoring empowerment highlights an immediate need to enhance ongoing efforts to strengthen poverty and welfare monitoring systems. However, despite the prominence of citizen empowerment, the action plan's detailing of ten critical areas of information gathering and analysis includes little mention of empowerment indicators or measurement. In addition, recent work undertaken for the World Bank's forthcoming Ethiopia Poverty Assessment demonstrated that direct indicators of empowerment are extremely hard to find.

Agency and Opportunity Structure

Many intermediate indicators of empowerment, especially indicators referring to a person's agency, are already generated by well-honed and tested questions in tools such as the LSMS and social capital survey tools. Rather than generating new indicators or survey questions, the draft module utilises indicators and questions that have already been developed. In both cases, existing sources of information or survey questions are identified. In addition to recognising the contributions of existing instruments, this approach reduces possibilities of duplication and enhances opportunities to easily integrate parts of the empowerment module into other national-level survey activities.

In the ME framework, opportunity structure comprises the presence and enactment of institutions, defined as the "rules of the game." Where possible, it also identifies sources that can be used for finding related data. Measuring institutions is complicated by the huge gap that exists between the presence of rules and the messy, politicised, and socially constructed reality of the enactment of those rules. Measurement of institutions will therefore require a mixed-methods approach that includes national-level tracking of legislation, regulations, and procedures and, ideally, local in-depth probing of the operation of informal institutions, or at least the specification of well-informed assumptions about the operation of informal institutions.

The framework proposed for measuring empowerment is a simple one. It comprises three core concepts: agency, opportunity structure, and degree of empowerment. These are further refined into clusters of indicators. The existence of choice, the use of choice, and the effectiveness of choice are used as indicators of the degree of empowerment a person or group experiences. For ease of data collection and analysis, three domains, State, market, society are identified and divided into a number of sub-domains, or stages in or upon which actors live out their lives. These sub-domains are differentiated according to the level at which actors operate—the macro, intermediary, and local levels.

Using this framework, empowerment can be measured within projects or interventions. It can also be used as the basis for in-depth research, for national-level monitoring, and, with certain caveats, for comparing the status of and changes in empowerment across countries. As demonstrated in the Ethiopia WDIP indicators empowerment is measured in five of the eight sub-domains, but in the Honduras Community-Based Education Project, empowerment is measured in only two sub-domains. How many domains an in-depth research exercise focuses on depends on the purpose of the study and the specific country context.

In contrast to the five ME studies, national-level tracking is not used for measuring the processes and impacts of a specific intervention. Rather, targeting a much wider group of stakeholders, it can be used to measure the empowerment status of a country's population. The national-level module, once refined, can stand alone or can be modified to work with other poverty or governance monitoring tools. The module will be piloted and amended over the next year.

Six key findings that have emerged during the development and preliminary effort to test the ME framework include:

First, is the ME framework's value for both analytic and applied purposes. Operationally, the framework has informed both the conceptualisation and the activities of two empowerment projects currently under preparation. In addition to using the framework to measure empowerment in six countries, it has also structured three country case studies on power, equality, and poverty, and the analysis of empowerment for one country poverty assessment.

Second, while providing very broad boundaries, the concepts of domains, sub-domains, and levels provide a pragmatic solution to the fact that degrees of empowerment vary according to what people are engaged in and where the activity occurs.

Third, the conceptualisations of assets and opportunity structure are useful for understanding the underlying reasons and dynamics that shape the degrees of empowerment of different actors, and for identifying activities and strategies for improving people's empowerment. Changes in assets or the opportunity structure are likely to precede changes in degrees of empowerment. Identifying asset and opportunity structure indicators is therefore also useful for evaluating intermediate impacts of investments in empowerment. Depending on the nature and components of the intervention, monitoring and evaluation teams have to decide whether they want to focus their studies on assets, opportunity structure, degrees of empowerment, or any combination thereof.

Fourth, distinguishing between different degrees of empowerment is important for two reasons. One, it helps to identify indicators that adequately reflect an empowerment outcome. Two, the distinction between different degrees of empowerment makes it possible to capture gradual advancements in the empowerment status of respondents.

Fifth, context-specific variables and values are important. Empowerment implies changing power relations among people or groups. As such, it is a relational concept, and neither the actors nor the relationships are likely to be the same in any two countries.

Finally, local definition of variables and values generates analysis that is of primary use within a single country. However, this does not mean that certain generalisations cannot be made about differences in degrees of empowerment among countries. Using the concepts of domains and levels, useful cross-country commentary is possible on the relative degree of empowerment of different groups, such as women or those traditionally marginalised.

This working paper is an interim product of a series of in-country efforts to measure empowerment. Five of these measuring empowerment studies have been synchronised and the teams linked through the development of the analytic framework and exchanges.

References

Davies, Martin (2002). *The Blackwell Companion of Social Work* (2nd ed.). Oxford, UK; Malden, MA: Blackwell.

Fischer, Joel and Kevin J. Corcoran (2007). *Measures for Clinical Practice and Research: A Sourcebook* (4th ed.). Oxford, UK; New York, NY: Oxford University Press.

Greene, Roberta R. (2008). *Social Work with the Aged and their Families* (3rd ed.). New Brunswick, NJ: Transaction Publishers.

Grinnell, Richard M. and Yvonne A Unrau (2008). *Social Work Research and Evaluation: Foundations of Evidence-Based Practice* (8th ed.). Oxford, UK; New York, NY: Oxford University Press.

3

Standards for Social Work Practice

Current and emerging advances in the science of genetics provide significant promise for enhanced health and well-being and an opportunity for social workers to make a major contribution. As rapid discoveries in genetics and genomics continue to identify genetic components of common diseases such as Alzheimer's, diabetes, cancer, heart disease, mental illness, and even behavioural characteristics, virtually everyone will be affected. Knowledge of the genetic make-up of oneself or a family member may present significant dilemmas and may lead to a serious consideration of alternative life plans. A genetic test can alert people to advanced detection and management of some disorders, but currently the ability to test for a genetic disorder often exceeds science's ability to prevent or cure genetic disease.

A social worker is often the first to provide psychosocial services to individuals and families with genetic disorders. Therefore, it is imperative that social workers become more aware of the ethical, legal and psychosocial implications of a genetic diagnosis, genetic testing and genetic research in order to empower individuals and families to speak out for their rights as public citizens. Without specialised training, it is inappropriate for social workers to assume the role of genetic counsellors, but they have important contributions to make within the social work scope of practice. Social workers can take an active part in ensuring that their clients are protected against genetic discrimination in areas such as health and life insurance, employment, and adoption. There are increasing opportunities for professional development of social workers in the field of genetics, and social workers should take the initiative to seek out those resources.

As critical issues are identified in the field of genetics, such as the benefits and risks of gene therapy, stem cell research, reproductive technology, and tissue cloning, social workers need to become more informed and sensitive to related ethical, legal, and psychosocial considerations to be helpful to their clients.

The ongoing knowledge explosion in genetics and its positive and challenging sequelae present considerable opportunities for the social work profession.

The National Association of Social Workers (NASW) recognises the need to integrate knowledge of genetics into social work practice in the context of the NASW Code of Ethics.

History of Social Workers and Genetics

For more than 40 years, social work as a profession has recognised the importance of genetic disorders in relation to social work practice and education. The Human Genome Education Model (HuGEM) project, funded by the National Institutes of Health and co-chaired by two social workers, offered workshops and training programs in genetics for social workers and other disciplines across the country from 1997 to 2001. NASW was an active participant in this project, which served as a catalyst for increased involvement in the field. The National Coalition of Health Professionals in Genetic Education (NCHPEG) was formed in 1996 and included two social workers representing both NASW and the Council on Social Work Education (CSWE) on its steering committee.

In addition to the efforts to improve social work education in genetics, the social work practice community has worked to clarify the social work role in genetics. An *NASW Social Work Practice Update* in 1998 defined the role of social workers in genetics, emphasising practice, policy, and ethical issues. The NASW policy statement on Genetics provided a framework all social workers could use to understand ethical and practical issues in genetic testing and research. In these NASW documents, it was made clear that social workers in all fields need to understand the ethical and practical issues involved with genetic testing. The Policy Statement included a commitment by NASW to continue work to establish the social work profession as a leader in the field of genetics, to support the development of programs, training, and information that provide social workers with current genetic information for use with clients, and to support policies that provide protection for clients from employment and insurance discrimination.

Goals of the Standards

These standards address genetics as an expanding field of knowledge for social workers and emphasise the need for clarification of, understanding of, and education about this specialised area.

The standards are designed to enhance social workers' awareness of the skills, knowledge, values, methods, and sensitivity needed to work effectively with clients, families, health care providers, and the community and to increase their understanding of the impact that the field of genetics has, and will have, on them.

The specific objectives of the standards are

— To inform social workers about genetics as an expanding field of social work knowledge

— To improve the quality of social work services provided to clients with genetic disorders

— To provide a basis for the development of continuing education materials and programs in genetics

— To ensure that social work services to clients with genetic disorders are guided by the NASW *Code of Ethics*

— To advocate for clients' right to self-determination, confidentiality, access to genetic services and nondiscrimination

— To encourage social workers to participate in the formulation and refinement of public policy relevant to genetic research, services, and treatment of populations with genetically identified predispositions or conditions.

(1) Standard 1: Ethics and Values

When integrating genetics and social work practice, social workers shall function in accordance with ethical principles and standards of the profession as articulated in the NASW Code of Ethics.

Interpretation

Social workers can make a significant contribution to the field of genetics by advancing a humane and ethical approach. Among the current ethical issues of relevance to the social work profession are

— Equitable access to genetic services, including testing and treatment and financial coverage for these procedures
— Privacy and confidentiality of individual genetic information, particularly in relation to the insurance industry and employers
— Self-determination, including allowing the client to select or refuse genetic testing and treatment in a noncoercive, unbiased manner.
— Informed consent, including protecting the right of the client to make decisions with regard to genetic testing and research based on a clear understanding of the risks and benefits
— Voluntary genetic testing and treatment
— Appropriate authority for genetic decision making on behalf of children and impaired adults
— Protection of the rights of those living with genetically determined conditions.

With its historic commitment to serving and empowering populations at risk and promoting human rights and social justice, social work is well suited to address the ethical challenges that arise from new genetic knowledge. The NASW Code of Ethics provides a philosophical framework for ethical social work practice and a set of ethical standards intended to define acceptable professional behaviour. Cultural competence is highlighted and practitioners are enjoined to provide culturally sensitive services. The client's right to privacy and confidentiality, self-determination, nondiscrimination, and social justice are clearly articulated in the Code. Genetic services should be interdisciplinary to achieve a holistic approach to client care. In this context, these standards address mutually respectful relationships among colleagues. The Code also acknowledges the complexity of ethical dilemmas, which defy simple answers. The Code suggests that the resolution of seemingly contrary mandates is best approached through a reasoned, systematic process that incorporates ethical theory and appropriate peer and interdisciplinary consultation and supervision.

(2) Standard 2: Genetics Knowledge

Social workers shall acquire a basic understanding about genetics as a science and a field of study, including its biological, psychosocial, ethical, and legal aspects.

Interpretation

Advances in the scientific understanding of the human genome leads to better comprehension of diseases, both common and rare, and ultimately leads to better diagnosis and treatment. Because of the rapid increase in genetic knowledge and because most social workers do not have a background in genetics, they need to gain a basic understanding of predisposition to common illness and inherited disease patterns. Social workers must continually update their understanding as new knowledge becomes available.

Social workers need to become familiar with general terminology used in human genetics and basic patterns of biological inheritance and with the role of genetic factors in maintaining health and preventing disease. It is important to include a relevant medical history in social work assessments in working with families. A family history is crucial in determining a genetic diagnosis and in predicting how various family members might be affected in the future.

Although new information on genetics has increased our understanding of the etiology of physical and mental illness, prevention and treatment of genetic disorders are very limited. This creates difficult dilemmas for people who are now in a position to decide whether to get tested themselves or to have their children tested. People who are at risk of genetic disorders will have increased options to use the new information to guide their reproductive behaviour. However, many of the possibilities raise serious moral questions.

As the genetic basis of common diseases becomes better known, it is especially important for social workers to become knowledgeable about indications for genetic testing and referral resources for such testing. In cases where genetic testing is available, social workers need to understand the potential benefits and risks of genetic knowledge to individuals, families, and communities Psychosocial reactions to genetic testing, cognitive responses, and coping strategies are important areas of knowledge for social workers, as are family issues.

A genetic test may provide people with information that can inform both their reproductive decisions and health behaviors. Because environment affects genetic expression, a genetic test may also alert people to a need to change their physical and social environments.

Genetic testing has an uneven history in the United States, and social workers need to be familiar with this and have an understanding of how genetic information can be beneficial or misused. Social workers working with clients should make efforts to keep current with legislative and legal developments through continuing education and in-service training.

Social workers need to be able to locate genetic resources in their communities and elsewhere. They need adequate understanding of genetic counselling and how it differs from other types of counselling. This knowledge is helpful in explaining to clients what to expect from genetics professionals and what to expect from social workers.

(3) Standard 3: Practice Skills in Working with Individuals, Families, Groups, and Communities

Social workers shall use appropriate practice theories, skills, and interventions that reflect their understanding of genetic factors in their work with individuals, families, groups, and communities.

Interpretation

Basic social work skills can be used to provide genetic services to individuals, families, groups, and communities. A professional commitment to continuing education in genetics is necessary for the integration of current and emerging genetic information and technology into appropriate social work settings. The social workers' biopsychosocial perspective is ideal for their role as liaisons between health professionals and clients, client advocates, and providers of psychosocial support services. The social worker should serve as an advocate for these clients, assisting individuals and families in adjusting to chronic health conditions, creating and maintaining appropriate self-help groups, resolving bereavement issues, and taking action at the community level regarding genetic privacy and potential discrimination.

More specifically, social workers should develop skills to

— Gather relevant genetic family history information, including a multigenerational family history that includes parents, children, siblings, grandparents, aunts/uncles, cousins
— Identify clients who might benefit from a referral for genetic services
— Properly communicate to clients the purpose of genetic services and the role of various genetic professionals
— Provide culturally sensitive services to clients with or at risk of genetic conditions
— Seek assistance from and refer to appropriate genetics experts and peer support resources
— Explore with clients the possible range of emotional effects they and family members may experience as a result of receiving or refusing genetic information
— Assist clients and their families in the genetic decision-making process, and in adapting to genetic information throughout the life cycle
— Discuss costs of genetic services and insurance benefits
— Discuss potential risks of discrimination in insurance, employment, adoption, and other areas
— Safeguard privacy and confidentiality of genetic information of clients to the extent possible
— Facilitate the creation and maintenance of support resources for genetic service clients
— Obtain current genetic information from reliable sources, for self, clients, and colleagues

— Educate clients, professionals and the community about policy issues regarding genetics
— Advocate for client-focused public policy in genetics.
— Assist clients in the understanding of the limitations and benefits of participating in genetics research and the importance of informed consent.

(4) Standard 4: Client/Practitioner Collaborative Practice Model

Social workers shall be able to work with their clients with genetic concerns in a partnership that includes mutual respect, shared information, and effective communication.

Interpretation

Individuals and families who have genetic concerns and those serving them have a shared commitment to quality services for everyone. Clients have expert knowledge of themselves and their family situations.

Social workers can be helpful to individuals and families in understanding the information they receive about their genetic make-up. Clients need to have a role in the collaborative team when choices regarding health care and other genetic services are being considered. Social workers should be aware of the psychological dynamics that individuals and families experience when making genetic decisions.

(5) Standard 5: Interdisciplinary Practice

Social workers shall participate in multidisciplinary teams that deliver comprehensive genetics services.

The complexity of genetic conditions requires a holistic approach to intervention. Individuals and families with genetic disorders, or at risk of them, need to receive services from a variety of health professionals working collaboratively to ensure optimal benefit. Multidisciplinary teamwork is central to the new, dynamic science of genetics.

By virtue of their education and training, social work professionals are well suited to working as part of a multidisciplinary team. Social workers have expertise in identifying and coordinating services and in bridging gaps in professional communication among service providers.

A common goal for all disciplines is to provide quality services to the population of affected persons and their families. In particular, all disciplines must be attuned to the emotional and social needs of individuals with genetic conditions. Healthcare professionals such as social workers, psychiatrists, psychologists, and nurses who provide psychosocial services to individuals and families can include genetic issues in these services.

Social workers, with a team approach, can establish bridges between clients and health professionals such as genetic counsellors, medical geneticists, and primary care physicians. In addition, the support group/professional partnership is essential in empowering individuals and families living with genetic disorders.

(6) Standard 6: Self-Awareness

Social workers shall have and continue to develop an understanding of their own personal, cultural and spiritual values and beliefs pertaining to genetics and genetic therapies.

Genetic knowledge and practices may conflict with basic beliefs, not only in clients, but in social workers themselves. To be able to effectively assist clients, social workers must continually examine their own backgrounds and identify their assumptions, values and beliefs related to human reproduction, medical intervention and the value of life with major disabilities.

Becoming a self-aware and self-reflective practitioner involves the examination of one's own bias about groups with views different from one's own. Social workers need to work to develop an understanding of different views, and to avoid judging clients with different values. There may be situations in which social workers will find themselves unable to empathise or remain objective. Self-awareness means taking responsibility for identifying such situations and working on one's issues so that they do not interfere with the client's decision-making. In instances where the social worker is unable to accomplish this, referral should be made to a social worker who can be neutral while assisting clients in this highly sensitive work.

(7) Standard 7: Genetics and Cross-Cultural Knowledge

Social workers shall have and continue to develop specialised knowledge and understanding about the history, traditions, values, and family systems of client groups as they relate to genetics.

Social workers need to possess specialised knowledge regarding the influences of their clients' ethnicity, culture, values, religious and health beliefs, and economic situations to understand their client's use of genetic information and services. The social worker will need to assess the meaning the client is placing on this concern. This process of cultural exploration is needed to assist in decision making regarding the pursuit of genetic information and later the results of that decision on the individual, the family, the community and the wider social context. NASW has developed NASW Standards for Cultural Competence in Social Work Practice that establish guidelines for practice (NASW, 2001).

There are many sociocultural barriers to genetic services. Social workers should use and promote the use of appropriate language and literacy levels when discussing genetic information with clients and their families. When taking a genetic family history, they should be culturally sensitive and aware of language and underlying emotional content. As a client advocate, the social worker must address genetic privacy and confidentiality of genetic information with an awareness of possible cultural meaning and social stigma for an individual or a group.

In summary, social workers may assist in overcoming cultural barriers to genetic services by

- Using and promoting the use of appropriate language and literacy levels when communicating with clients and their families in regard to genetic information
- Being culturally sensitive in obtaining a genetic family history

— Being aware of cultural factors in working with individuals and families regarding the genetic decision making process and in adapting to genetic information
— Addressing genetic privacy and confidentiality of genetic information with an awareness of possible cultural meaning and social stigma for an individual or a group
— Advocating for cultural competence in service delivery and throughout the health system

(8) Standard 8: Research

Social workers shall contribute to, support, and be cognisant of the development of research-based and practice-relevant knowledge of the psychosocial, cultural, economic, and ethical implications of genetics on individuals, families and society.

Much remains to be learned about how to promote the well-being of individuals, families and society in the context of the genetic revolution. Research is needed on how individuals and families react to learning about their genetic risk status, how they make decisions based on that knowledge, and how society can ensure that genetic information is used for the common good. Research can inform our understanding of how genetic information may differentially affect the diverse cultural and ethnic groups within our society, and how to be culturally sensitive to these differences.

Social work's "person-in-environment" perspective can make a unique contribution to the understanding of the impact of genetic information on our society. Social workers are ideally suited to observe the impact of genetic information on individuals, families, and society; draw preliminary generalisations; and form theories that may be tested in research studies to enhance social work practice.

Social work research must be guided by basic ethical and cultural principles, as defined by the Code of Ethics of the National Association of Social Workers (1999). Promotion of the well-being of the client is the primary responsibility of the social worker. Informed consent, the equitable selection of subjects, privacy and confidentiality, the right to withdraw from studies, and avoidance of harm are among the standards that are essential for ethical research studies. The consequences of research must be considered, and appropriate institutional review boards consulted in the early stages of project development.

(9) Standard 9: Advocacy

Social workers shall safeguard the privacy and confidentiality of genetic information of their clients and advocate for and with clients when appropriate to ensure fair social policies and access to quality genetic services.

Social workers are keenly aware of the importance of maintaining their clients' privacy with regard to genetic information, as well as the potential for discrimination based on that information and the need for social advocacy and social action to better empower clients and communities.

To protect clients, social workers must be aware that there are limitations to the confidentiality of genetic test information. Insurance companies, employers, the criminal justice system, and other government agencies have enormous financial incentives to gain access to people's genetic information. Of particular concern to social workers is the potential for labelling individuals and withholding services from those with genetic conditions.

The right to confidentiality extends to both the decision whether to be tested and the decision of who is allowed access to the test results. Social workers should inform clients about the possible disclosure of confidential information and the potential consequences before the disclosure is made.

Social Work Guiding Principles

The constant growth, demands, and changes in health care have had a serious impact on the viability and need for social workers in all areas and settings of health care. More than 15 percent of the population or 45 million people in the United States were without health insurance coverage during 2003. Access to timely, comprehensive, and equitable health care for individuals in the United States varies considerably, with significant percentages of many populations having only limited access to health care. The growth in medical technology has offered hope and improved quality of life to many people; yet, the advances in technology have also raised health care costs and introduced social, legal, and ethical dilemmas for individuals, families, and health care providers.

Currently, health care social workers provide services across the continuum of care and in various settings. Social workers are present in public health, acute, and chronic care settings providing a range of services including health education, crisis intervention, supportive counselling, and case management.

The health care system in the United States is complex and multidisciplinary in nature, and may include a network of services such as diagnosis, treatment, rehabilitation, health maintenance, and prevention provided to individuals of all ages and with a range of needs. Multiple sources of financing, ranging from Medicare and Medicaid to private insurance, provide further challenges. Many consumers lack health insurance or have inadequate coverage, which causes financial stress on consumers and providers.

Professional social workers are well equipped to practice in the health care field, because of their broad perspective on the range of physical, emotional, and environmental factors that have an effect on the well-being of individuals and communities. The National Association of Social Workers (NASW) recognises that standards alone cannot improve the quality of practice unless they are disseminated and implemented at the practice level. Client satisfaction and improved quality of care result when social workers and administrators recognise and use these standards.

Social workers have been involved in the health care field since the turn of the 20th century. The profession's earliest concerns were with making health care services available to the poor and with improving social conditions that bred infectious diseases such as tuberculosis. Today, social workers can be found in every component of the health care system. In 1977, NASW published Standards for Hospital Social Services. In 1980, the Standards for Social Work in Health Care Settings were developed and replaced the hospital standards. Between 1981 and 1982, the NASW Board of Directors approved the new standards, and three subsections were developed, approved, and added to the health care standards.

In the early 1980s, a capitated system for payment of Medicare services in acute health care settings, known as diagnostic-related groups (DRGs), was initiated by the federal government. This initiative, generically known as managed care, fundamentally altered health care financing for both public and private health care systems. Managed care focused on reducing the length of stays in acute care facilities, and this led to a fundamental shift in the role of social workers in acute health care. Yet, in other settings, social workers have prospered, gaining recognition through the provision of specialised services in multiple health care arenas such as palliative care, ethics, ambulatory care, rehabilitation, and geriatric services.

The NASW Standards of Social Work Practice in Health Care Settings are based on the consensus of expert health care social workers from across the country and are designed to enhance social workers' knowledge, skills, values, and methods necessary to work effectively with individuals, families health care providers, and the community when practising in health care settings.

The basic values of social work, from promoting an individual's right to self-determination to having an attitude of empathy for the individual, are the foundation of social work practice.

Social workers have skills in cultural awareness and cultural competence, in which social work practice respectfully responds to, and affirms, the worth and dignity of people of all cultures, languages, classes, ethnic backgrounds, abilities, religions, sexual orientation, and other diverse features found in individuals (NASW). Social workers practice at the macro and micro level of health care and thus have the ability to influence policy change and development at local, state, and federal levels and within systems of care. Social work research in health care benefits not only individuals and families, but also the very existence, effectiveness, and validation of the profession. These standards offer a guide for social workers practising in any health care setting.

Definitions

(i) Bioethics

Bioethics is the analysis and study of moral, legal, social, and ethical considerations involving the biological and medical sciences. Many health care settings have organised forums such as bioethics committees, institutional review boards, or consultation processes to address ethical dilemmas and questions.

(ii) Biopsychosocial–spiritual Perspective

The biopsychosocial–spiritual perspective recognises that health care services must take into account the physical or medical aspects of ourselves (bio); the emotional or psychological aspects (psycho); the sociocultural, sociopolitical, and socioeconomic issues in our lives (social); and how people find meaning in their lives (spiritual). This approach draws from the strengths perspective of social work practice.

(iii) Case Management

Case management, sometimes used interchangeably with care management, is the collaborative process of assessment, planning, and facilitation for options and services to meet an individual's complex needs. When appropriate, this would include arranging, coordinating, monitoring, evaluating, and advocating on behalf of the client and/or his or her family for the multiple services needed from a variety of social service and health care agencies.

(iv) Client/Patient/Consumer

These terms refer to the person receiving care and treatment from physicians and allied health care personnel. Social workers generally use the term client to identify the individual, group, family, or community who seeks or is provided with professional services. The client is often seen as both the individual and the client system or those in the client's environment.

(v) Continuum of Care

The care continuum includes the specialised health, social work services, rehabilitative, and home-based services that a seriously or chronically ill or injured person might need.

(vi) Continuity of Care

Continuity of care ensures the coordination of care within an organisation or across different agencies or settings to reduce duplicate services, to address gaps in existing services, and to ensure consistent and continuous services for the client as they transition in care or are discharged.

(vii) Disabling Condition

A disabling condition is considered a temporary or permanent reduction in a client's capacity or functioning based on the inability to perform some activities that most others can perform.

(viii) Health Care Settings

Health care settings are practice areas in which assessment, care, and treatment address the physical, mental, emotional, and social well-being of the person; and address prevention, detection, and treatment of physical and mental disorders with the goal of enhancing the person's biopsychosocial and spiritual well-being. The health care setting includes personnel who provide the necessary services: and educational and environmental facilities that work to help prevent disease.

(ix) Health Planning

Health planning is conducted in government organisations, medical and research organisations, and educational institutions and in prevention, early intervention, treatment, and follow-up. Planning should involve determining and ensuring the number of necessary health care personnel presently and in the future, and how to both finance and control costs.

(x) Managed Care

Managed care is a process designed to manage health care costs primarily through the private sector, although Medicaid's or Medicare's capitated systems are a form of managed care. It is a technique used by insurance carriers and characterised by pre-authorisation to qualify the patient for particular services; preauthorisation for a given amount of care; review of treatment and patient response(s).

(xi) Medicaid

Medicaid is a government-funded health insurance program that provides payment for hospital, nursing home, home care, dental, and medical services to people who meet disability guidelines and income eligibility requirements. The Medicaid program is a shared federal/state/county program and although there are certain federal standards, states have a choice of benefits which they can choose to cover or not.

(xii) Medicare

Medicare is a national health care program, administered by CMS, for most people age 65 and older, people with a variety of disabilities who are under age 65, and people with end-stage renal disease (ESRD), which is permanent kidney failure requiring dialysis or a kidney transplant (CMS). Medicare is funded through a combination of employer–employee contributions, from earmarked taxes, and general federal revenues. Since Medicare is a federal program, benefits are the same in all 50 states.

(xiii) Public Health Model

The Public Health Model of services focuses on the health of the individual, the family, and the larger community or general public and is administered by federal, state, and local agencies. The goal of programs, policies, and health care personnel is to prevent and treat disease, identify and eliminate environmental hazards, prolong life, and promote better health.

Standards for Social Work Practice in Health Care Settings

(1) Standard 1. Ethics and Values Social Workers shall have Knowledge of and Practice Acc ording to the Guidelines Established by the NASW Code of Ethics (NASW).

The primary mission of the social work profession is to enhance human well-being and help meet the basic human needs of all people, with particular attention to the needs of people who are vulnerable, disenfranchised, oppressed, and living in poverty. These core values, embraced by social workers throughout the profession's history, are the foundation of social work's unique purpose and perspective:

— Service
— Social justice
— Dignity and worth of the person
— Importance of human relationships
— Integrity
— Competence

In a health care system increasingly driven by technological advances, the ethical and moral questions and dilemmas raised for clients, families, and health care professionals are numerous and complex. Ethics committees are often used to provide "objective" reviews to health care providers and clients and families, when there is conflict between providers or providers, clients, and families. Institutional review boards are used to protect clients from the potential of experimentation in research projects. Social work supervision and peer consultation can also be used to discuss ethical issues facing practitioners.

(2) Standard 2. Health Disparities Social Workers Practising in Local, State, National, and International Health Care Settings require Knowledge and Skills to help them Recognise and Address Inequalities and Injustices Directed toward Clients, Organisations, and Communities related to Access to Care and Provision of Health Services.

Many social workers have historically delivered services as part of community-based organisations and public health programs to address health disparities among those who are least likely to be able to gain access to adequate care. Social workers have an ethical obligation to address the health care needs of these groups and advocate for change to ensure access to care. Training of health care professionals to achieve a level of cultural competence is an essential part of basic and continuing education for all health care professionals, including social workers.

Health is a matter of both economics and social well-being. Both domestically and internationally, health care social workers strive to gain knowledge about health care. Social workers also help clients to gain access to health care as they navigate between and among complex service delivery systems and entitlements.

Different entities shape public and global policies in every country. Therefore, social workers must keep abreast of policies to competently help clients and to assess physical, environmental, historical, situational, cultural, and structural factors that affect health care systems.

Accessibility to preventive, palliative, and curative health care depends largely on the client's ability to pay, and often, people cannot afford existing fees. In many non-profit community-based clinics, services are provided on a "first come-first serve" basis and are limited by a shortage of supplies and equipment. Increasingly, private systems of care emerge alongside public systems and other health care providers to care for the uninsured or underinsured who need health services, yet prefer to care for those who can pay fee-for-services.

(3) Standard 3. Cultural Competence Social Workers shall Develop and Maintain an Understanding of the History, Traditions, Values, and Family Systems of Client Groups as they relate to Health Care and Decision-making. In Compliance with the NASW Standards for Cultural Competence in Social Work Practice (NASW), Social Workers shall have a Sensitivity to and Awareness of the Diversity in Cultural Groups and Integrate this Knowledge into their Practice.

The importance of recognising, respecting, and understanding other cultures and related health beliefs lays a foundation to build therapeutic alliances with clients and families.

Social workers in health care shall approach each client and family interaction from a perspective of cultural respect and awareness. This implies reluctance to stereotype individuals based on assumed group similarities and seeks instead to ask individuals what aspects of their cultural experience are meaningful in understanding a particular health care need.

Appreciation of cultural influences is especially important for clients at critical health junctures, such as birth, diagnosis of a major illness, and facing the end of life. Social workers have a responsibility to assist the client and family system in observing culturally meaningful practices whenever possible. When delivering culturally competent services, social workers should be guided by the NASW Standards for Cultural Competence in Social Work Practice (NASW).

(4) Standard 4. Confidentiality Health Care Social Workers shall Maintain Appropriate Safeguards for the Privacy and Confidentiality of Client Information.

Social workers must be familiar and comply with local, state, and federal mandates related to confidentiality. Professional judgment in the use of confidential information shall be based on best practice, ethical, and legal considerations. Clients, families, and other professionals should be informed of the confidentiality limitations and requirements before services are initiated and in all phases of the health care experience.

(5) Standard 5. Knowledge Social Workers in Health Care Settings shall Demonstrate a working Knowledge of Current Theory and Practice and Integrate such Information into Practice.

The social worker uses knowledge about, and psychosocial implications of, illness, injury, and health conditions to provide social work services to clients and families to help them manage and cope with the impact of such health matters. Social workers have expertise in communication; navigating systems of care, resources, client and family coping skills; and the comprehensive impact of health conditions on the client.

Essential areas of knowledge and understanding about health care include:

— The roles and functions of social work in health care

— The biopsychosocial needs of clients and families

— The physiological elements of illness and their impact on psychosocial functioning

— The psychological and spiritual needs of clients and families and how to ensure that they can be addressed

— Community resources to assist clients and families

— The disparities across cultures and economic groups in gaining access to and funding for health care

— Ethical and legal questions and dilemmas

— Laws, regulations, and policies affecting clients, families, and social work practice

— The accreditation and regulatory standards governing settings providing health care
— Evidence-based practices and social work research in health care
— The needs of special populations.

(6) Standard 6. Assessment Social Workers shall Provide Ongoing Assessment, including Gathering Comprehensive Information to Use in Developing Interventions and Treatment Strategies.

Assessment is a fundamental process of social work practice. Treatment and intervention strategies/plans require that social workers both assess and reassess client needs and modify plans accordingly. Social work assessments in health care settings include considering relevant biomedical, psychosocial, and spiritual factors and the needs of the individual client and the family (NASW).

A comprehensive, culturally competent assessment includes:

— Past and current health status including genetic history of family health
— The impact of health conditions or treatments on cognitive, emotional, social, sexual, psychological, or physical functioning
— The impact on body image, intimacy, and sexuality
— Social history, including current living arrangement and household environment
— Work, school, or vocational history
— Stage in the life cycle and related and relevant developmental issues
— Cultural values and beliefs, including views on illness, disability, and death
— Family structure and the client's role within the family
— Social supports, including formal and informal support systems
— Behavioural and mental health status and current level of functioning, including history, suicide risk, and coping styles
— Financial resources, including access to and type of health insurance.

(7) Standard 7. Intervention and Treatment Planning Social Workers implement Intervention and Treatment Plans that Promote Client Well-being and Ensure a Continuum of Care. Planning shall be Based on a

Comprehensive, Culturally Competent Assessment with Interdisciplinary Input.

Intervention and treatment plans are steps identified by the health social worker, in collaboration with the client and with other members of the team, to achieve objectives identified during assessment. Social workers shall be able to adapt practice techniques to best meet client needs within their health care setting to work effectively with individuals across the life-span, with different ethnicities, cultures, religions, socioeconomic and educational backgrounds, and across the range of mental health and disability conditions (NASW).

Intervention or treatment plans may include:

— Strategies to address needs identified in the assessment
— Information, referral, and education
— Individual, family, or group counselling
— Vocational, educational, and supportive counselling
— Psychoeducational support groups
— Financial counselling
— Case management
— Discharge planning
— Interdisciplinary care planning and collaboration
— Client and systems advocacy
— Goals and objectives.

(8) Standard 8. Case Management Social Work case Management shall Optimise Client functioning. Case Management Facilitates Collaboration among Providers to Address the Client's Biomedical and Psychosocial needs to better Provide Efficient, Appropriate, and Beneficial Health Care Services to a Client with (often) Multiple Needs.

Social work case management requires the professional social worker to develop and maintain a therapeutic relationship with the client, which includes linking the client with resources that provide a range of services, resources, and opportunities to enhance successful quality outcomes for the client. Case management may include having regular meetings with the client and family and assisting the client to navigate systems.

The scope of services would include the following:

— Psychosocial assessment, including diagnoses, interventions, and treatment plans
— Financial assessment, planning, and intervention
— Case facilitation
— Patient and family counselling
— Crisis intervention
— Quality improvement
— Resource brokering/referral/development
— Continuity of care planning
— System integration
— Outcome/practice evaluation
— Teamwork/collaboration
— Patient/family education
— Patient/family advocacy

(9) Standard 9. Empowerment and Advocacy Social Workers have a Responsibility to Advocate for the Needs and Interests of Clients and Client Systems in Health Care, including Advocating for Larger System Change to improve Access to Care and Improved Delivery of Services.

Social workers have a special responsibility to advocate for the needs of the disenfranchised or the most vulnerable of the population at both the micro and macro levels. Social workers will identify barriers to services and actively seek to resolve them.

(10) Standard 10. Client and Community Education Social Workers act as Educators for Clients, Families, the Community, and Other Professionals regarding Disease Prevention, Impact of Illness and Disease Progression, Advocacy for Benefits, Health Maintenance, and Adherence to Treatment Regimens.

Social workers have a formal role as educators. Social workers gain knowledge and expertise in the health practice setting from other professionals and from formal education, work, or teaching experience. They have the knowledge and skill to implement the principles of learning theories in education programs, activities, and resources. They communicate and collaborate with departments and other staff to foster client education.

Social workers use a variety of methods to define and identify learning needs of individuals and families. Assessment identifies the educational needs based on the expressed needs of individuals, family members, and significant others. Social workers collaborate with the health care team to design educational activities to meet the client's needs, to deliver the activities in a method that facilitates the learning needed, and to evaluate the process in an integral, ongoing, and systematic manner.

(11)Standard 11. Teamwork and Collaboration Social Workers shall Participate in Care Teams, and Collaborate with Other Professionals, Volunteers, and Groups in and Outside of their Practice Setting to Enhance All Aspects of the Client and Family System's Care.

Social workers participate in multiple care teams, which are typically interdisciplinary. These teams often provide comprehensive care and information in a client's home, in outpatient or inpatient health, and mental health care settings.

As part of such teams and collaborations, social workers shall demonstrate the ability to:

— Understand the mission and functions of the service organisation or group for which the social worker is employed
— Understand the role of other relevant professions and organisations
— Communicate and cooperate appropriately with other disciplines and agencies
— Ensure that the social work role and responsibilities are clearly delineated and communicated to other members of the team
— Ensure that the roles and responsibilities of each collaborating organisation are clearly delineated and communicated
— Advocate for changes in care that reflect the interests of the client and client system
— Communicate the client's information in a respectful and objective manner and protect the client's confidentiality and privacy

— Share leadership and decision-making functions

(12) Standard 12. Workload Health care social workers shall maintain a workload that allows for efficient and quality social work service delivery. The size of the social work staff shall represent the scope and the complexity of the organisation and the nature and numbers of the populations served.

Both the health care organisation or setting and the social work leader and staff have joint responsibility for establishing and maintaining a workload that allows for adequate and appropriate interventions and monitoring of services and outcomes. The workload also reflects the demands of the population served and may include social work coverage outside of regular office hours. It is the joint responsibility of the organisation and the social worker to resolve issues of workload concerns.

(13) Standard 13. Documentation Social Workers shall Maintain Records or Documentation of Social Work Services, which Reflect the Client and Client Systems' Pertinent Information for Assessment and Treatment; Social Work Involvement and Outcomes with and for Clients; and in accordance with Care Goals and Legislative and Administrative Regulations and Policies.

The importance of clear, concise, and organised documentation reflects the hallmark of quality social work services and often serves as the mode of communication between a social worker and other professionals and clients. The elements and responsibilities of thorough and comprehensive documentation include the following:

— Comprehensive assessment and services delivered to the client and client systems, including the development of a plan of care

— Ongoing assessments, interventions, and treatment planning

— Goals and planning that reflect an explicit statement of agreement with client, client systems, and team input

— Referral sources and collaborations

— Dates, times, and descriptions of client and client system contacts

— Documentation of outcomes

— Reason for case closure or transfer
— Written permission to release and obtain information, where appropriate
— Documentation of compliance with confidentiality rights and responsibilities
— Documentation of receipts and disbursements

(14) Standard 14. Research Health Care Social Workers shall Understand Research Planning, Methodology, Evidence-based Outcomes, and Program Evaluation.

Social workers have a responsibility to be familiar with the literature crucial to their area of practice. As professionals, social workers in all settings have a mandate to improve the knowledge of the field, and this can best be accomplished through participation in research activities.

Venues where health care social workers might help to develop, implement, or evaluate research include inpatient and outpatient hospital-based settings, community or home health agencies, and federally funded clinical trial research networks.

Clinical trials help answer scientific questions and greatly depend on study participants' committed participation. Social workers may help physicians, nurses, pharmacists, and others recruit individuals and encourage study participation and adherence to medication regimens; they can also help clients manage problems that may hinder adherence and retention, such as challenging life circumstances and demands from family members.

(15) Standard 15. Performance Improvement Health Care Social Workers shall be a part of Ongoing, Formal Evaluation of their Practice to Assess Quality and Appropriateness of Services, to Improve Practice, and to Ensure Competence.

Social workers are trained to facilitate improvements that alter the processes in which health care is delivered. They are ethically charged to promote process improvements that will enhance patient or consumer safety, satisfaction, efficient and effective care, and identify and promote best practices and equitable care on a multidisciplinary basis.

The evaluation of social work practice is a vital part of social work service delivery. The methods to evaluate such practice include peer review, self-evaluation, supervision, and other research methods. Evaluation practices may include the following:

— Using appropriate tools such as clinical indicators, practice guidelines, consumer satisfaction surveys and measures, and standardised performance assessments
— Assessing both outcome and process objectives
— Involving the client and client system and colleagues in the evaluation process
— Protecting the privacy of the client and client system and other professionals
— Disseminating evaluative data to clients, payers, and other professionals on request and adhering to privacy rights
— Using external practice evaluators as appropriate
— Participating in social work research.

(16) Standard 16. Access to Information and Technology Health Care Social Workers shall have Access to Computer Technology and the Internet, as the Need to Communicate Electronically and to Seek Information on the Web for Purposes of Education, Networking, and Resources is Essential for Efficient and Productive Practice.

Health care professionals, including social workers, communicate, learn, educate, and document using computer technology on a daily basis. Social workers need initial and ongoing training in technology applications relevant to their practice, including clinical care, research, policy, education, resource finding, and administration.

Standards for Professional Development, Education, and Leadership

(17) Standard 17. Qualifications Health Care Social Workers shall meet the provisions set for Practice by NASW. A Sufficient Number of Qualified Social Work Personnel shall be on Staff to Plan, provide, and evaluate Social Work Services.

Health care social workers shall have a social work degree from a school accredited by the Council on Social Work Education (CSWE). As a distinct speciality within the social work profession, health care social work requires specialised knowledge as outlined in these Standards. The social worker should receive this knowledge and skill set from involvement or internship in a health care setting, preferably under social work supervision.

Social workers functioning in leadership roles, such as managers or directors, should be licensed at the advanced practice level and able to provide supervision for licensure.

(18) Standard 18. Continuing Education Health care Social Workers shall assume Responsibility for their Own continued Professional Development in accordance with the NASW Standards for Continuing Professional Education (NASW, 2002) and state requirements.

Social workers shall remain knowledgeable about medical diagnoses and advancements, and the psychosocial implications of illness, injury, disability, and treatment.

Social workers shall assist in identifying health care and psychosocial topics for professional development by participating in research; by encouraging organisations and institutions to collaborate, advocate, and provide appropriate education for the field; and from clinical practice.

(19) Standard 19. Supervision A Social Work Leader or Supervisor shall be available to supervise Health Care Social Work Staff on their Responsibilities in Practice, Research, Policy, Orientation, and Education.

The purpose of supervision is to enhance the clinical social worker's professional skills and knowledge, to enhance competence in providing quality patient care. Supervision aids in professional growth and development and improves clinical outcomes. Experienced social workers shall offer guidance and consultation to students, interns, and less experienced peers.

(20) Standard 20. Leadership Social Workers across all Health Care Settings have a Responsibility to provide Leadership to ensure access to Care and to improve and Maintain the Quality of Care provided by an Agency or Institution. Leadership Skills can be demonstrated in Teams

and Groups across Health Care Settings, and include monitoring Others within and Outside the Social Work Profession.

Social work leaders typically demonstrate knowledge, skills, and abilities in the following areas:

— Management/administration, which includes supervision, consultation, negotiation and monitoring

— Specialised knowledge of how to function within care teams in which various disciplines are involved

— Research and education

— Legal, ethical, and professional standards applicable to health social work practice including standards of documentation (paper and computer) and quality improvement activities

— Ability to priorities needs for social work services and to recommend adjustments to staffing levels accordingly based on current literature and industry standards

— Social work qualifications, productivity, and continuing education

— Policies and regulations that affect social work practice, and patient and family care

— Information on access to health care for the underserved and marginalised populations

— Consultation to social workers and allied health professionals on relative health social work practice issues

— Development of and adherence to organisational policies, procedures, and regulations by staff.

References

Specht, Harry; Courtney, Mark E. (1994). *Unfaithful angels : how social work has abandoned its mission* New York: Free Press.

Statham, Daphne (2004). *Managing Front Line Practice in Social Work.* New York, NY: Jessica Kingsley Publishers.

Thyer, Bruce A. and John S. Wodarski (2007). *Social Work in Mental Health: An Evidence-Based Approach.* Hoboken, NJ: John Wiley.

Turner, Francis J. (2005). *Canadian Encyclopedia of Social Work.* Waterloo, ON: Wilfrid Laurier University Press.

4

Delivery of Social Services

The delivery of basic services is a central task of poverty reduction. Poor people say that water, education, healthcare and personal security are among their highest priorities, and expanding inclusive service delivery is critical to achieving the Millennium Development Goals.

Strategies to improve service delivery typically emphasise the central role of the state in financing, providing, and regulating services. The state bears the legal responsibility to ensure that the fundamental human rights to security, education, and healthcare are realised. The state is also well placed to respond to the challenges of scale and market failure in ensuring access for services to all groups.

But how should services be delivered where the state is unable or unwilling to take up its responsibilities? State weakness or fragility can occur in many ways. Sophisticated strategies to improve the relationship between state regulators and private providers have little relevance where the government is repressive or lacking commitment to poverty reduction goals.

In difficult environments, donors and other international agencies have tended to withdraw. While humanitarian assistance and limited support to state or non-state actors are important, the prevalent donor response has been to curtail development efforts until the capacity and willingness of the state return to 'normal'. But donor disengagement over the years in places such as Afghanistan has shown that long-term state weakness carries a heavy price in terms of sowing the seeds of its own endurance.

Service Delivery in Difficult Environments

The importance of remaining engaged despite the difficulties involved. *Department for International Development* (DFID) considers continued involvement in service delivery of vital importance for four reasons:

— The Millennium Development Goal (MDG) targets represent a global commitment to realising the rights of the poor to services and livelihood opportunities.

— There is a 'humanitarian imperative' to respond to an emergency situation where people's access to services has been severely reduced or has completely diminished.

— Service delivery may offer an entry point for triggering longer-term pro-poor social, political and economic change.

— Service delivery may help to prevent some states from sliding (back) into conflict by addressing its structural causes.

Rights and the MDGs

The world is off track to reach the Millennium Development Goal (MDG) targets for primary education, gender equality and maternal and child mortality. The MDGs reflect the multidimensional nature of poverty and are at the centre of DFID's development work. The goals also represent a collective commitment from the international community to ensure that the rights of the poor to education, health and a decent standard of living are met

Making better progress in difficult environments represents one of the biggest challenges to achieving the MDG targets. Using low scores on the World Bank Country Policy and Institutional Assessment (CPIA) indicators a proxy for difficult environments, more than 40 countries with the lowest scores over the last five years are home to an estimated 343 million people living on less than $1 per day. This is 59% of all absolute poverty outside India and China. Again, leaving aside India and China, the same states account for approximately:

— 49% of maternal deaths,

— 54% of people without access to safe drinking water,

— 51% of children out of primary school and
— 58% of people living on less than a dollar a day.

Meeting Urgent Humanitarian Needs

Donors provide humanitarian assistance in difficult environments because of their commitment to an impartial humanitarian response and allocation of funding according to need. INGOs and UN agencies with a humanitarian mandate are key providers of services in many situations where political will is lacking or where there is ongoing conflict. To maintain their operating space, these agencies work within humanitarian principles of neutrality, impartiality, and independence.

Humanitarian interventions are effective at meeting immediate needs, but may be less so at facilitating longer-term systems building. This is because humanitarian aid is designed to bypass host governments in order to rapidly and effectively relieve human suffering.

Service Delivery as a Catalyst for Longer-Term Pro-Poor Social, Economic and Political Change

Service delivery interventions can provide an entry point and trigger for longer-term pro-poor social, political and economic change in difficult environments. A pro-poor social, political and economic environment is one in which poor people are empowered to demand their rights and the state is responsive to the voices of the poor. Clearly, many of these conditions do not exist in difficult environments. Changing the situation is likely to require sustained engagement over time and it is hypothesised that service delivery provides one possible entry point.

The provision of basic services has the potential to break the inter-generational cycle of poverty and increase economic opportunity. Women's literacy has the potential to be a particularly powerful tool for social and political change if approached in the right way. Healthier and better-educated individuals are more likely to be able to build their livelihood opportunities, contribute to long-term economic growth, and protect themselves from economic shocks.

Service delivery can mitigate social exclusion particularly in marginalised areas such as slums and poorly communicated territories by the existence of mechanisms that reach down to community level and give the poor voice and the opportunity to participate politically. The Chars Livelihood Programe in Bangladesh has developed a useful conceptual model of how service delivery interventions can incorporate opportunities for the poor to exercise their voice, create political space, and, in the long term, fundamentally alter their relationship with elite groups.

Service delivery interventions can offer an entry-point for broader governance reforms. Where upstream governance weaknesses or lack of capacity are a contributory factor, the governance reforms that are necessary to promote longer-term social and political change have more chance of success if linked to reforms in service delivery, which have tangible results and benefit the public in a way they notice. Service delivery reforms could offer a more promising entry-point for broader governance reforms, if they are visible to the public as this can then lead to pressure for wider more systemic reforms.

Addressing the Structural Causes of Conflict

The structural causes of conflict are the long-term factors underlying violent conflict. There is an extensive literature that has sought to understand the causes of conflict, and the type of response that is appropriate. Analysis indicates that a range of social, political and economic factors are involved and interact in complex ways. What can be said with some certainty is that conflict reduction interventions are very cost effective, and that service delivery is an important part of the response. Below are some of the ways in which service delivery can reduce conflict.

Service delivery interventions may act as a tangible peace dividend in countries emerging from conflict. A number of service delivery interventions have been designed and implemented to reach down to the grassroots level help to stabilise the situation in the immediate aftermath of conflict. Interventions are sometimes referred to as 'quick wins' or 'quick impact' projects (QIPs). Several agencies employ quick impact type projects. They tend to tackle high visibility problems and to try to win 'hearts and minds'. In some cases, they are the precursor to more developmental approaches, centred on community-based reconstruction.

The literature on the role of 'horizontal inequalities' in conflict highlights the importance of considerations of equity in the provision of services. Horizontal inequalities can be defined as inequality between groups in society rather than between individuals. This work argues that group exclusion along social, economic, and/or political lines is a source of differentiation and is one of the potential triggers of conflict. Access to services is one of the factors contributing to such differentiation.

Education can be crucial in addressing the underlying causes of conflict in terms of its structures and systems and curriculum content. In countries emerging from conflict, education is frequently regarded as having a crucial part to play in rebuilding social cohesion. Systemic approaches are necessary, which tackle participation and transparency in policy formulation, equitable distribution of resources, curriculum reform, and other exclusionary tendencies. In a conflict situation, education can be a means of creating a peaceful space and offering children a 'normal' experience in an otherwise crisis situation. The school curriculum can conversely be used as a vehicle to incite ethnic and racial hatred.

Challenges to Supporting Pro-poor Service Delivery

Service delivery as a relationship of accountability between users, providers and policy-makers. The World Development Report 2004 proposes a possible framework for conceptualising pro-poor service delivery that examines the relationships of accountability between the policy maker, the provider and the citizen.

This framework has been criticised for being too narrowly focused on accountability as the primary mechanism for improving the responsiveness of frontline providers. Other important contributing factors include human resource capability, the role of civil society organisations in advocating for the rights of the poor to basic services, and the role of trade unions and other professional organisations in working with their members to improve the quality of service provision.

In a 'good' policy environment, the international community seeks to partner predominantly with policy makers at the state level to strengthen the state's ability to monitor and build the capacity of providers to work with poor citizens to give them more voice to demand their right to health, education and other services from the state through 'voice initiatives', and to build the responsiveness of providers to citizens by finding mechanisms for citizens to directly hold providers to account. Poverty Reduction Strategies provide the framework for this engagement.

The WDR's analysis provides only a partial answer to the question of what to do in situations of state weakness or failure. The WDR framework 'Eight sizes fits all' suggests that the path to take in situations where the state is not pro-poor is to strengthen client power, through some form of direct transfer of funding, either from central government or from donors. However, the model does not address the challenge of (re)building effective state institutions in situations where these have deteriorated, have been destroyed by conflict, or are depleted by HIV/AIDS.

Some difficult environments are characterised by a lack of political will, which means that policy makers and politicians will not push forward a pro-poor agenda. For the international community, a balance needs to be struck between using diplomatic tools to influence governments, and ensuring that the humanitarian needs of vulnerable groups are met. In some instances, particular groups may be deliberately targeted by repressive regimes.

Many difficult environments, the state may lack the capacity to supply services to poor people. There are frequently very weak policy making, implementation and monitoring systems, a lack of organisational providers and frontline workers, and limited financial resources. Whilst this may be true of many developing countries, in difficult environments the problems may be particularly acute and are exacerbated by such factors as limited access to certain parts of the country because of challenges of geography or security. In these situations, it will be difficult for the government to supply medicines or textbooks in some areas, and teachers, doctors and nurses may be reluctant to work in remote or inaccessible regions.

The complex interplay between political will and state capacity poses major obstacles to poor people's access and participation in service delivery in difficult environments. Where political will is lacking, certain groups may be deliberately excluded from social services on the basis of gender, ethnicity, religion, caste, tribe, race, or political affiliation. In situations of weak state capacity the poor may be unable to access services because of their geographical location, or because the services available do not meet their needs or have high real and/or opportunity costs.

Pro-poor Service Delivery

In difficult environments scaling up the delivery of services and reaching the poor is problematic because the relationships between the policy maker, the provider and the citizens break down. The state is unwilling and/or unable to monitor and support providers or to respond to demands from citizens for service access and quality. Given these challenges, this section considers what approaches are available for the international community to:

— Strengthen pro-poor policy making functions

— Build provider capacity

— Reduce barriers poor people's access and participation

Strengthening Pro-poor Policy Making Functions

Policy maker functions include setting policy, regulating and monitoring the implementation of policy through the compact with providers, striving to meet the rights of citizen's to basic services, and ensuring that there is sufficient financing to implement policy.

(i) *Find entry points to build pro-poor political will*: Lack of willingness is unlikely to reflect a uniform decision about implementing policy goals across the whole of government. There may be pockets of political willingness in certain central ministries, or in elements of local government.

(ii) *Strengthen capacity of state policy making functions*: where there is some state willingness, efforts to build policy making and implementation capacity are best directed at the state and state structures because this is where ultimate responsibility for pro-poor service delivery lies. Support for the state can occur at central planning and financing levels, at the sectoral level, or at decentralised levels of government. Decisions as to where to engage will depend very much on analysis of capacity and will at the different levels. Approaches to building state capacity include providing long-term technical assistance, supporting elements of recurrent expenditure, and financing community recovery through decentralised structures. Engagement in capacity building requires a long-term commitment from the international community. Policy based interventions aimed at supporting the public sector in difficult environments pose several challenges for the international community.

(iii) *Use non-state mechanisms for policy coordination*: in environments where there is unwillingness on the part of government, or where capacity is so weak as to make a sector or sub-sector dysfunctional, then it may be necessary to consider alternative mechanisms for coordinating policy, at least in the short to medium term. Mechanisms may be necessary at the central level, at the sectoral or thematic level, and/or at the sub-sectoral level. Effective coordination may also be undermined by the motivations of different agencies, and the lack of 'teeth' in coordination mechanisms to ensure that all agencies participate.

Reduce the risk of undermining the state. Where possible, even if alternative mechanisms are used, relationships with the government and with state structures should be maintained in order to facilitate possible handover back to full state oversight. Otherwise there is a danger of creating completely parallel structures that undermine the state's ultimate responsibility for service delivery. Social funds, for example have been criticised on the grounds that they sometimes fail to build local and central government capacity and they may have poor coordination in the targeting of service delivery interventions. The risk of undermining the state can be reduced by aligning donors' systems with government financial systems by sharing a common policy framework as far as possible, and by not unnecessarily weakening state capacity though drawing away key human resources.

Building Capacity of Service Providers

Service providers include organisational providers frontline professionals and the organisations that support these professionals. In difficult environments, the capacity of providers may be weak in terms of infrastructure, human and financial resources, and responsiveness to the poor.

Build capacity of state providers: in situations where there is some willingness and capacity, state providers should be considered as an entry point for strengthening service delivery. This is for two reasons. First, it can be an effective way of building state accountability for public services, and second it is less likely to undermine an already fragile state. The key challenge is to work with the state to find ways to make limited human and financial resources extend the reach of services to the poor.

Many countries, particularly across sub-Saharan Africa, are facing a growing crisis of human resource capacity, which is significantly impacting on their ability to deliver vital public services. The problem is particularly stark in difficult environments where, conflict may exacerbate overall shortages of personnel, teachers and health personnel may be unwilling to work in remote areas, and there are high levels of absenteeism. In situations of crisis, there is a need for immediate or shorter-term radical and innovative solutions to boost the capacity for delivering services. Developing longer term solutions will need to include changes in incentives around pay, morale and motivation, effective and active management, and transparent employment systems.

(i) *Harness non-state providers*: in areas where there is no government provision, and no prospect of building the capacity for government provision in the short to medium term, then the international community should consider harnessing non-state providers in ways that do not undermine the state. One possible way to do this is through some kind of contracting arrangement. Contracting potentially allows governments, and those acting to support them, to harness the capacities of both state and non-state providers for service delivery, while simultaneously introducing an accountability mechanism through performance or output based contracts. Contracting is important because it offers prospects for scaling up the response through non-state actors. Evaluations have been conducted in post-conflict Cambodia.

(ii) *Working with humanitarian agencies*: INGOs and UN agencies with a humanitarian mandate are key providers of services in many difficult environments. Most implementing agencies operate within the core humanitarian principles of neutrality, independence and impartiality. There is a long history of efforts to align humanitarian efforts more closely with development efforts, particularly with regard to the challenge of 'post conflict' reconstruction. This is because an overemphasis on commodity driven approaches that bypass government structures and fail to build local capacity makes it much more difficult to re-engage developmentally when there is a resolution to the crisis.

More recently, academic think tanks, funding agencies, and implementing agencies, have all been involved in re-examining and rethinking the concepts of humanitarian and development aid, the links between them, and also the links between them and diplomatic and military responses. This renewed interest has been partly fuelled by a recognition that humanitarian crises can continue for many years, by a widening of the concept of what constitutes a country in crisis, and by an increasing acceptance that humanitarian aid fundamentally has a political dimension.

There are serious challenges to making closer links between humanitarian and development actors. The possible erosion of the principles of neutrality and independence may increasingly lead to humanitarian agencies becoming the target of belligerents in conflict. Also, the challenge of developing more coordinated approaches to service delivery in emergency situations should not be underestimated as several recent evaluations of coordinating mechanisms highlight. Finally, getting humanitarian actors to agree on a common approach is a major difficulty as they approach the issues from divergent positions and differ significantly with respect to their ethos, size and motivations.

Reducing Barriers to Poor People's Access and Participation

Poor people lack access to services in difficult environments for a number of reasons. These include deliberate social exclusion, remote geography, inappropriate services, high real and/or opportunity costs, or security concerns. While many of these obstacles are also present in 'better performing' environments, they are magnified in the types of context under discussion here.

1) *Strengthen the voices of the poor and vulnerable*: voice refers to the relationship between the citizen and the politician. It is the mechanism through which the citizen demands of the policy maker his/her rights to services. Strengthening voice is essential to longer-term transformational change, and may be achieved in tandem with efforts to develop improved mechanisms for service delivery.

However, in many difficult environments the conditions for mobilising voice may be weak or absent. Sierra Leone is an example of the common failure to respond to the voice of girls and women in countries emerging from conflict. Interventions that have the strengthening of voice as their primary objective face a dilemma in many difficult environments. While voice is a key to long-term social and political change, it can be a dangerous entry point in repressive environments where government may see community mobilisation as a threat to their power base. Decisions as to the balance between direct service provision and mobilisation activities need to take account of the social and political context.

2) *Move resources to community level*: community based approaches are an entry point to set up local governance structures, which can then act as a focal point for service delivery interventions. The demand generated is then directed at some kind of social fund, umbrella grant, or dedicated government funding mechanism to which communities can direct proposals for project funding. Funds may be administered through local government structures if these have the capacity and legitimacy, or they may sit completely outside of government. NGOs and smaller CBOs play a role in either implementing sub-projects, or in community mobilisation activities.

3) *Facilitate provider access*: a major challenge in all difficult environments is gaining and maintaining access for service providers to the poor and vulnerable. In conflict-affected areas, an issue is one of security for service providers. The approach to this

problem in Nepal, where the Maoists and the security forces often block access, is to work through basic operating guidelines. These guidelines have been agreed by the international community and guide agencies with respect to their behaviour in the field. They incorporate fundamental humanitarian principles and call on the parties to the conflict to comply with their obligations under International Humanitarian Law. This brokering role is a key one for the international community to play, and in situations of crisis it may involve invoking humanitarian law and seeking to get monitoring missions on the ground to hold state and non-state forces accountable for their actions.

4) *Reduce the costs of accessing services*: one challenge for the poor in difficult environments is meeting the cost of accessing services, both direct and indirect. There are strong advocates for the removal of user fees in the health and education sectors, but this may not be feasible in many difficult environments where non-state actors are a major provider of services, and lack of government capacity makes effective regulation virtually impossible. More promising may be efforts to increase the amount of disposable income that the poor have access to. One way to do this is through cash for work programes.

Understanding of Context is Crucial

It is critical to understand the capacity and will dimensions of difficult environments in order to inform programming decisions, and to minimise the risk of aid doing more harm than good.

+ WILL

Will but limited capacity	Will and capacity
Policy maker • Partner with central government and line ministries to develop, implement and finance pro-poor policy	*Policy maker* • Strengthen government system to develop pro-poor policy, monitor the compact, respond to voice, and be accountable to citizens
Provider • Encourage partnerships between the state and non-state providers	*Provider* • Build organisational and frontline provider capacity and provide incentives

• Build state provider capacity where possible	for frontline workers • Work to make providers more responsive to the poor
Poor people • Strengthen the voice of poor people to demand their rights to services • Use community based approaches that work through central and local government structures and link to sector interventions • Facilitate provider access	*Poor people* • Build client power and voice
- CAPACITY	*+ CAPACITY*
Limited will and limited capacity	Capacity but lack of will
Policy maker • Use non-state mechanisms for policy coordination	*Policy maker* • Use non-state mechanisms for policy and financing coordination and look for entry points to support political will
Provider •Deliver services through humanitarian agencies and INGOs in ways that build capacity and institutions where possible	*Provider* • Harness both state and non-state providers through some form of partnership arrangement
Poor people • Use community based approaches that build local governance structures and community capacity to manage their own service delivery needs • Facilitate provider access	*Poor people* • Use community based approaches that build local governance structures and develop community capacity to manage their own service delivery needs • Facilitate provider access

- WILL

Possible approaches to strengthening service delivery relationships and actors in difficult environments

The mapping is necessarily crude, and is certainly not meant to be prescriptive. It gives an indication of how entry points and approaches are affected by the type of context in which the international community operates. Environments that exhibit both capacity and will are included for comparison purposes. One country context may exhibit all four characteristics simultaneously.

Tools are needed to derive relevant contextual information and to agree on ways to pool and share it. In order to programe effectively, managers need a consistently excellent understanding of the context in which they are working. Arriving at an understanding of the capacity and willingness dimensions of any particular context will require the development of indicators and a methodology for applying them.

Making Trade-offs Explicit

Difficult environments force trade offs between short and long-term objectives. The short-term objective of the international community in difficult environments is to relieve immediate humanitarian suffering by providing life saving support, including delivering services. In the longer term, the objective is to facilitate social and political change that results in an environment where poor people are empowered to demand their rights and the state is responsive to the voices of the poor. These objectives frequently conflict with each other.

The kinds of approaches that are suggested in the top left quadrant clearly show that these environments are closer to 'business as usual' than either of the situations where there is a lack of willingness. The most difficult of this group of environments are those that are emerging from conflict and where the international community is seeking to legitimate a nascent government. One of the key issues here is to find ways to rebuild the system in ways that do not simply reproduce and reinforce previous inequities, or replicate dysfunctional alignments and institutions. Finding the right balance between 'upstream' reforms and making sure that services reach people on the ground is also a key issue.

In situations where there is government unwillingness but there is strong capacity, then finding an entry point for service delivery interventions in partnership with the state is extremely challenging. This situation is represented by the bottom right quadrant. In these situations, political analysis will be essential to identify opportunities for building political will. Policy coordination may need to be undertaken by a structure parallel to government, but where possible with connections to government structures. A careful balance needs to be struck between supporting the delivery of services and working with civil society organisations to mobilise communities to demand their rights to services. If not carefully managed the latter may result in conflict between citizens and the incumbent regime.

In situations where there is a lack of government will and state capacity, the community offers the most promising entry point for sustainable service delivery interventions. This is the situation represented in the bottom left quadrant – many of these contexts are conflict affected. The analysis draws attention to the need for parallel policy making structures and the importance of international humanitarian actors as providers of services in these environments. Sustainability and legitimacy may be less important than the humanitarian imperative to quickly get life saving services to poor and vulnerable people. The challenge is to do this in ways that build capacity for longer-term development through the development of local community structures and civil society actors. Community based approaches are a key part of the response.

Using Aid Approaches and Instruments Flexibly

Related to the above, is the need to have flexibility in the aid modalities at our disposal in difficult environments. Countries will typically exhibit varying degrees of capacity and willingness at any one time, and over time. It is clear that a 'one size' fits all approach will not work in these contexts. Table 1 summarises the main approaches, the common aid instruments for delivering this assistance, and the trade offs with respect to short and long term objectives:

Table 1. Approaches and trade offs

Approach	Possible Modality	Short term	Long term
Building capacity	DBS/SWAPS	Fiduciary risk Finance may get stuck upstream government and fail to reach the poor	Strengthens government legitimacy where this is a primary objective
Working through non	Multi donor funding	Can be effective at reaching the poor	Financing bypasses the state and may undermine it in the

state coordination mechanisms	arrangements Global Funds		longer term
Quick wins/ quick impact projects	Project support	Can reach down to pockets of the poor, but tends not to be systematic and difficult to scale up	Means of demonstrating political willingness in difficult environments?
Building capacity of non state actors	Contracting	Effective and efficient way to provide services in low capacity environments Provides a framework for monitoring outcomes	State legitimacy may be undermined Risk of elite capture of resources
Humanitarian interventions	Consolidated AppealsProcess	Effective at meeting immediate needs of affected populations	Bypasses government system and may not build capacity for the future Response can be become fragmented in the absence of strong coordination
Community based approaches	Social funds Umbrella grants	Effective way to move resources down to community level Puts power into the hands of the community	Risk of elite capture of resources Scaling up can be difficult Links to sectors may be problematic
Voice only initiatives	Civil society funds	Risk of backlash from a repressive regime No immediate return with respect to access to services	Builds social cohesion and puts power in the ends of the poor Powerful tool for promoting social, political and economic change

The current range of instruments may not be sufficient to deal effectively with difficult environments. Current aid instruments may not be optimally effective. Activities that assist in delivering essential services to the poor, especially regarding HIV/AIDS are among the eligible activities. Though the total size of the Trust fund is relatively small, this instrument has enhanced the Bank's ability to help meet some needs in the most difficult environments.. There are likely to be others, including instruments to support interventions that fall somewhere between humanitarian and development responses.

The international community, funding agencies and implementing agencies alike, have very limited evidence as to the impact of their service delivery interventions in difficult environments. It has proved extremely difficult to find empirical support in the existing literature for the extent to which service delivery interventions impact on human development outcomes or promote longer-term social and political change. Rigorous evaluation of existing instruments and approaches will assist in arriving at the optimal mix of modalities for any particular context.

Improving the Humanitarian/development Transition

Where possible the international community should seek to work with humanitarian actors to better coordinate their activities, to develop a more pragmatic and strategic vision of service delivery, building local capacity where appropriate.

Humanitarian actors should further develop ways of programming that maintains humanitarian independence and impartiality but makes the transition to longer-term development less difficult. Partnerships between humanitarian and development actors at the implementation stage could be strengthened. The objectives of development and humanitarian agencies in the field also need to be better aligned and this can be facilitated by attempts to improve specific aspects of the response, such as UNHCR's durable solutions initiative.

Implementing Promising Approaches

Difficult environments present challenges to scaling up the delivery of services to the poor, but the analysis does suggest some promising approaches. Although the evidence base on impact is weak, there are some indications of how the international community can increase its engagement in the support of service delivery in difficult environments in ways that both improve human development outcomes and lay the seeds for change in the future. Any efforts to increase funding must be accompanied by a thorough analysis of the possible unintended consequences.

Supply side approaches include the following.

— Contract out service delivery to non-state actors in situations of weak state capacity. This approach has been applied successfully in the health and water and sanitation sectors, and it could be extended to the education sector. Output-based contracts outline a minimum package of services and the desired outcomes in terms of service access and impact on the MDGs.

— Scale up through a non-state mechanism where there is a lack of political will. One option is to use the UN as a lead organisation to manage service delivery in these contexts.

— Explore new ways of working for both humanitarian and development agencies; humanitarian agencies will need to engage more fully with the long-term role of the state in service provision, and to develop a broader more flexible and less commodity-driven range of instruments for social protection.

On the demand side, approaches include the following:

— Work through civil society organisations to empower the poor to demand their rights to services. This is effective where there is capacity to deliver and where political judgment indicates that the regime will not regard this as a threat.

— Move resources down to community level through local committee or similar structures. Communities themselves can then make decisions about where to target resources.

References

Mizrahi, Terry and Larry E. Davis (2008). *Encyclopedia of Social Work* (20th ed.). Washington, DC; Oxford, UK; New York, NY: NASW Press and Oxford University Press.

Popple, Philip R. and Leslie Leighninger (2008). *The Policy-Based Profession: An Introduction to Social Welfare Policy Analysis for Social Workers* (4th ed.). Boston, MA: Pearson/Allyn and Bacon.

Reamer, Frederic G. (2006). *Ethical Standards in Social Work: A Review of the NASW Code of Ethics* (2nd ed.). Washington, DC: NASW Press.

5

Social Services of General Interest

In general the scope as described by the communication is recognised and found appropriate and adequate. Social services of general interest are those services that make a right effective. Some contributors underlined, like the communication, that the role of social services is not limited to assistance to the most vulnerable groups but concern the social protection of the whole population and that these services also play a preventive role. Social services of general interest (SSGI) address the whole population and are related to the realisation of social policy goals and objectives.

Most respondents feel that the EU should not try to come to a definition of SSGI. Like for services of general interest in general this definition role belongs to the competent national authorities. Moreover, for some contributors it is not desirable to distinguish a specific category of SSGI since SSGI are not different from other services of general interest. It is argued that a distinction between SSGI and SGI might lead to more confusion.

Others emphasise the need to establish a clear distinction between SSGI that cannot be classified as economic activity and therefore are not submitted to competition and internal market rules and SSGI which are of an economic nature but nevertheless, because of their specific features, require that these rules should be applied in an appropriate manner.

Some contributions point out that statutory social security schemes should be presented separately since these have been clearly recognised as non-economic by the European Court of Justice but others do not agree with this separation. Other contributions mention that the division between social security schemes and social services is not always clear. Statutory and complementary social security schemes are not in themselves social services, but are implemented by these services.

The exclusion of health services from the scope of the Communication appears as a concern for many contributors. Some point out that the Communication still covers health since it specifies that social security schemes covering the main risks of life, including health are SSGI. Others highlight the thin line and the complementary aspects between social and health services and regret the separate treatment. Also, it is argued that the objectives and modes of organisation of health services are similar to the ones of social services. Most contributors state that coherence with the health initiative must be guaranteed and a common approach would be preferable. Some of these contributors feel however that a common approach would only be needed in specific areas.

Also, regarding social housing, a much broader approach should be taken, encompassing the part played in promoting a socially mixed society. More attention should also be paid to job training for members of vulnerable groups and to services specialised in employment for handicapped people.

Notion of General Interest

Almost all contributors agree that there is no general definition of the general interest. The general interest is defined by the national public authorities responsible for the service. It was recalled that several aspects relating to the general interest are defined at Community level. Even though, some contributions mentioned that it would not be meaningful to try to define the general interest at the European level. Some contributions reported that services of general interest are determined by law, also when provided at the municipal level. The content of the term depends on the content of the respective Act. First, the general interest is defined and then the ways how to implement it are worked out.

Many elements of the expression of the general interest have been reported: it includes the provision of services targeted to the society as a whole; it refers to services provided or funded by the State, semi-governmental organisations and NGOs; it is carried out in light with public interest, profit is secondary. Other key elements listed are the objectives of a social nature the link with public funding, the implementation of the principle of solidarity, accessibility, availability, equal access and equal terms, democratic control. In the field of social services the general interest must take into account the welfare state principles which are based on constitutional rights. Indeed, most Member States' constitutions state that (minimum) conditions for an existence in dignity should be guaranteed.

PROPOSED CHARACTERISTICS

First of all, many contributors confirm that the characteristics applying to services of general interest do apply to social services of general interest. However, some contributions have pointed out differences in the application of these principles to social services. They argue that the universality of a service does not relate to social services which are provided to particularly disadvantaged groups and this type of service should be tailored to the needs of the beneficiary.

Continuity should also be understood in a special way. Network services should be provided continuously, while certain social services should be provided with no interruption in periods when they are needed. Affordability and accessibility should be understood with regard to price maintaining and guarantees for the most vulnerable.

On top of that, the specific characteristics for SSGI, which cannot be described as simply "organisational", are recognised by most as pertinent to gauge the specific features of social services of general interest, even if some feel it has to be made clear which characteristic applies to which of the two groups of social services as described in the April 2006 Communication. Moreover not all of the organisational characteristics apply to all the social services.

Comments made on Each Proposed Characteristic

To synthesise the main issues at stake, it is proposed to go through each of the characteristics listed in the Communication with a description of the comments received. The characteristics are presented according to the pertinence the respondents attribute to them.

(i) *They operate on the basis of the solidarity principle, which is required, in particular by the non-selection of risks or the absence, on an individual basis, of equivalence between contributions and benefits.*

It has been mentioned that the operation on the basis of solidarity is the main characteristic of SSGI. Social justice has also been mentioned as a mode of operation of SSGI. From these principles of solidarity and social justice derive important specificities of SSGI: the risks they cover are not individual but structural, as they offer wide protection without being selective or discriminating.

However, it was also pointed out that social services do not operate exclusively on the basis of the solidarity principle, but also on the basis of welfare principles, whereby access to other social welfare services is often subject to a means test or assessment of the specific need.

(ii) *They are comprehensive and personalised integrating the response to differing needs in order to guarantee fundamental human rights and protect the most vulnerable.*

While the importance of the link between fundamental human rights and social services is acknowledged, it is often pointed out that this characteristic mixes two different notions and is formulated in a too restrictive way. Social services of general interest while aiming at protecting the most vulnerable and ensuring the equal dignity of all human-being- do not only address the need of the most disadvantaged people but base their work on a universalistic approach. It is a fundamental right for everybody to have access to the appropriate social services. In the meantime, the vulnerability of certain users of social services has been highlighted as distinguishing them from normal consumers. It was also highlighted that personalisation implies the integration of different services. Finally, it has been mentioned that person-oriented social services often address not only the physical and mental needs but also the spiritual aspect of care for each human being.

(iii) *An asymmetric relationship between providers and beneficiaries that cannot be assimilated with a 'normal' supplier/consumer relationship and requires the participation of a financing third party.*

The asymmetric relationship and the often vulnerable position of the beneficiaries are acknowledged. The asymmetric relationship is moreover expressed through the fact that users find themselves in circumstances outside one's control. This underlines the need to put an emphasis on quality.

Some contributions mention that there is generally no direct link between the actual cost of the service provided and the financial contribution of the user, but also that there is not always the participation of a financing third party.

Three types of reactions can be distinguished:

1. For many contributors the non-for profit nature is not a distinguishing characteristic. There should be no limits or preferences regarding the form of ownership of the providers of SSGI as long as the service providers comply with the service (quality) requirements and guarantee an effective provision.
2. It has often been mentioned that whatever the nature of the provider (for-profit or not-for profit), profit is not the main purpose of providers delivering social services of general interest.
3. Other contributors would like to enlarge the reference to public authorities, organisations close to public authorities with a specific public status, charity or welfare organisations, churches or their organisations, associations, mutualities, cooperatives or organisations consisting of volunteers.

(v) *They include the participation of voluntary workers, expression of citisenship capacity.*

The contribution of volunteers in the provision of certain social services of general interest is recognised, however, its importance varies across the EU. It is also mentioned that some social services of general interest do not necessarily include the participation of voluntary workers and often require highly skilled workers. Volunteers should not be singled out as an exclusive characteristic.

Meanwhile, other contributors would like to reinforce this characteristic by adding that volunteering is an added value for both the user as well as the volunteer, promotes active citizenship and social inclusion, as well as social cohesion and the creation of social capital. The importance of professionalisation of workers in social services is also stressed.

(vi) *They are strongly rooted in (local) cultural traditions. This often finds its expression in the proximity between the provider of the service and the beneficiary, enabling the taking into account of the specific needs of the latter*

The notion of proximity is largely recognised. For some, the service provider must be familiar with the customs, standards and traditions in order to provide the service to the user in the most suitable way.

Proposals for Additional Characteristics

Finally, some contributions have proposed additional characteristics to highlight the specificities of social services of general interest:

— They work with the capacity of the user and assist him/her to become independent.
— The aspect of universal access should be further stressed
— They often include an element of advocacy in order to defend the interests of the beneficiary and to work for social justice in society;
— They are provided according to the wishes and the personal choice of the beneficiaries;
— They should rely on a multidisciplinary approach towards the beneficiaries and should be flexible;
— They place an important emphasis on users' rights. Indeed, the ability of the individual to participate in the choice of provider and method is important for a satisfactory result from the service;
— As the user of social services holds a weaker position and the provision of service deals with the questions concerning a

person's life arrangements, the existence of a quality monitoring and assessment system is extremely important, especially the existence of ex-ante verification and the possibility to authorise service providers.

— They affect the recipient and his or her integrity personally, which imposes special requirements as to the provision of these services;

— They often concern acute needs that must be met;

— They imply an active role of local communities in their set up, management and organisation;

— The providers of social services of general interest often operate in a democratic and autonomous manner involving the participation of their beneficiaries in the decision making process regarding both the general planning of services and the provision of services to a specific person;

— The recognition of the right of initiative of the providers and the recognition of the existence of providers created specifically to cover certain services, for instance in the area of social housing.

— They imply government regulation and planning related to the identified needs

— Funding can be public or private but is dedicated to social rights. Financing through taxes and/or compulsory social contributions;

— The existence of an act of power or authority which specifies the general interest objectives to be achieved by the service and the means for doing it

— Regarding the personal social services
  - Developed by the State or, in the framework of public-private partnerships, by private non-profit social solidarity institutions, recognised by the State which would be responsible for technical supervision and monitoring, financial support, and quality control for the services provided
  - Fulfilling a role of prevention and support to social inclusion

Some contributors stated that discussion should focus not only on how they are organised. Some also mentioned that the purpose of SSGI and the outcomes they achieve are more important and would provide a more straightforward basis for a common description. In this light, the following characteristics have been proposed:

— In addition to meeting the needs of a specific person, the universal availability of services also aims at guaranteeing the fulfilment of social policy objectives and the general good. Social services react to social needs and problems which occur because services in the market are not effective enough.

— They meet the social needs of societies, groups or individuals and which national, regional and/or local authorities consider to be essential in the light of the general interest. Social services seek to provide security and equal opportunities for all and social policy is also about redistribution between rich and poor, between those who are employed and those who are not, between young and old, between families with children and families/persons without etc.

Characteristics at National and EU Level

Respondents are divided on the need and the use of characteristics. Many respondents are against the use of characteristics at EU level mainly for reasons of subsidiarity and because of the high diversity in the organisation of social services at the Member State, regional and local levels. For most of those in favour of the use of characteristics at EU level, they should be used in a non-binding manner at EU level and serve as guidelines for Member States when defining and organising their social services of general interest.

For those against the use of characteristics at EU level, the main reasons are as follows. The definition and organisation of social services is a national or local responsibility and there is no need to fulfil it with EU wide characteristics. Therefore, there is no need for EU action until issues in the management of national processes are identified by Member States. Moreover, the proposed characteristics are too narrow to encompass the diversity across the EU, the role of market mechanisms and free choice. There is a need to agree on terminology first. Finally, for some respondents, social services are not legally different from services of general interest and there is no need for separate definitions.

For those in favour, characteristics defined at EU level could provide a basis for a clear distinction between services of general economic interest and social services of general interest and be therefore a tool for better clarity. Moreover, they could serve as guidelines for the definition of social services of general interest and their compliance with EU rules ie, the non cumulative characteristics would be used as a "cluster of evidence". For instance, when drafting a mandate to attribute a mission of social general interest to a service, Member States could refer to the characteristics to clarify the mission.

Finally, also for those in favour of non-binding EU characteristics, some clear restrictions have been highlighted. These characteristics should be flexible as the sector is evolving and defining social services of general interest remains a Member States competence. Furthermore, the characteristics should not overrule the variety of social services requirements which are the result of a long-term democratic policy process reflecting the population needs more than a legal process.

For some contributors, the characteristics proposed are too narrow to encompass the diversity of situations across the EU. The examples of child care and care for the elderly have been used to illustrate this point.

One example is child care. Across the EU there is general agreement on the need for societies to provide child care to families/individuals and there is therefore not much discussion about the general interest and the social character of these services. However, there are across the European Union many different ways in which child care is organised and provided. Child care services for instance do not necessarily include the participation of voluntary workers, and also are not exclusively provided by non-profit organisations. Also, not all child care providers deliver on the basis of solidarity and they not always require the participation of a financing third party.

Another example is elderly care; in this case as well the general character of this type of services is recognised. Elderly care is serving the needs of a general public and not necessarily only the most vulnerable. Indeed, as all people grow older, these services serve a very large part of society. They are provided by public, non-profit as well as profit-based organisations. The character of the elderly care sector has also recently changed significantly because of population ageing, the shift in working patterns of women, and the increase in the number of single elderly persons. Some of the services include the participation of voluntary workers.

Link with the Services Directive

For some, the Services Directive goes some way to recognise the special nature of social services. For instance, the special role of the State as mentioned in the Services Directive could be a good starting point for differentiating social services from services of general interest. Others highlight however that the framework of the Services Directive is not suitable for creating a reasonable balance between opening up the market for SSGI and the provision of the users' rights and needs.

Some contributors state that the relation between SSGI and the Services Directive is clear, but other contributors find the exclusion of certain social services from the Services Directive vague and feel it creates confusion.

Certain contributors feel the Communication could be a helpful basis for further interpretation of the scope of the exclusion. Some contributors feel however that the political compromise on the Services Directive should be respected and that there should be no attempts to interpret this Directive through other instruments.

Moreover, the exclusion in the Services Directive should match the scope of social services mentioned in the Communication and the characteristics should apply to the exempted social services.

Others think however that the characteristics are not suitable for defining the scope of SSGI which are exempted from the Services Directive and point to the fact that SGI are already exempted. The characteristics are too limited and cannot be used to exclude or include specific social services in the scope of the Services Directive. For some, the principles in the Services Directive are more in line with describing SSGI by their purpose than are the characteristics used in the Communication. Others consider the exemption from the Services Directive is in line with the characteristics identified in the communication.

APPLICATION OF COMMUNITY LAW

In general, contributions have mentioned that EU rules should take account of SSGI specificities and that the general interest should be reinforced in the body of EU rules and prevail in case of conflict with EU rules.

One Member State indicates that there are no problems as such with the application of Community rules, but in some concrete cases the question arises to which extent the Community rules give enough room to allow for a smooth transition of public towards private provision.

Public Procurement

Regarding public procurement, the issues highlighted are threefold: how public authorities prepare tenders, the consequences of public procurement procedures on the providers and on the users.

First of all, public authorities doing public tenders in the field of social services are facing many difficulties according to the responses to the consultation. Drafting tenders is reported as being a difficult and demanding task. Indeed, public authorities have difficulties to define the content of the services and to develop requirements in a detailed way all the more that the services will have to be personalised to the specific needs of each user. These difficulties are reinforced by the fact that public authorities do not necessarily know in details the needs and specificities of social services. Therefore, the risk of public tenders focusing on prices has been often mentioned. In this respect, the new EU public procurement regulations allowing for social, employment, ethical as well as ecological considerations to be taken into account has been welcomed and considered as an important step forward. However, it is now important that the inclusion of social, employment, ethical and ecological considerations is also transposed into national legislation. Moreover, the difficulties in drafting public tenders taking account of all important criteria pose a risk for the quality and the social efficacy of the services.

Furthermore, the public procurement rules are seen as not flexible enough regarding inter-municipal cooperation. For some contributors, inter-municipal procurements need to be removed from the scope of application of the Procurement Directives. Intermunicipal cooperation on a social service aiming at attaining a sufficient population base is made more difficult or even impossible by the public procurement legislation. In order to obtain a sufficient population base, small municipalities often need to cooperate with large municipalities in order to be able to provide certain social services. According to contributors, under the procurement legislation it is not possible for a smaller municipality to purchase these services directly from a large municipality nearby.

Moreover, contributors point out that some public authorities do apply public procurement rules even when not necessary or in a restrictive manner to be sure to comply Community rules. Therefore, a clearer communication on the application of public procurement rules is requested by some contributors.

In addition, a need for clarification of the obligations deriving from the principle of openness has been expressed. The Treaty presupposes that the principle of openness must be observed in purchases that are not covered by the scope of the Directive on public procurement. However, the application of this principle is subject to interpretation.

Finally, one contribution has highlighted the possibility to reconcile the pursuit of the general interest and public procurement procedures. Under the process for UK public sector procurement, the structure of the specifications takes into account the wider Government objectives.

Secondly, the issues related to providers revolve around the administrative burdens placed on small organisations, the risks of important concentration moves leading to monopolistic situations, and the changing relationship between the providers and the public authorities, the risks on the right of initiative of providers being one illustration.

Contributors indicate that providers have experienced increased paperwork in the last few years, manifold bureaucratic requirements for applications and reporting. These increased requirements bind a lot of valuable resources of organisations, which is especially difficult for small NGOs.

Furthermore, the application of public procurement is reported as changing the traditional type of relationship between public authorities and providers, for instance in Germany from cooperation to regulation of competition.

Thirdly, regarding the users of social services, the main issue reported is the lack of choice of the provider. The individual's choice of the method of care or provider of a social service is made difficult by public procurement legislations. Indeed, under a tender selection process only one provider is chosen.

In the light of these issues, the positive effects of public procurement applied to social services are questioned by some contributors. If the market functions well, competition may contribute to making the activities more effective and to cost savings, but there are several problems in the field of social welfare and health care that are caused by market failures, such as asymmetric information. Services must also be ensured in situations where the service concerned only is needed for a few users.

Public-private Partnerships

Regarding public-private partnerships (PPP) the main comments relate to the need for clarification at EU level of the rules: how an institutional public-private partnership should be implemented? What is the applicable law to PPP and to institutional PPP? In social housing, there are uncertainties on the status of PPP of certain mixed operations. These issues should be debated in the framework of the Green paper currently under review.

The issues reported on public-private partnerships are linked to the fact that public procurement is needed. Therefore, some of the problems exposed in the previous part are also applicable: the freedom of choice of citizens should be taken into account; cooperation with private actors like NGOs is reported more difficult as it needs to go through public procurement first. Therefore, for some contributors, cooperation between municipalities should not fall under EU law and PPP should be excluded from public procurement rules.

Internal Market Rules

In the field of freedom of establishment and freedom to provide services, the issues reported relate to unclear rules, the scope of the Services Directive and the application of internal market rules.

Concerning the need for clarification, to be compatible with EU rules, all measures aiming at regulating the market must be "proportionate".

On the Services Directive, the current wording of the exclusion of social services from the Directive is said to be vague and to create confusion about which services are covered by the Directive and which are not and are therefore covered by the Treaty dispositions on internal market.

On the application of internal market rules, the will to suppress the obstacles between Member States and the barriers considered discriminatory for the operators from other Member States induces a risk of questioning the national regulations framing the activity of social and health services and of non taking into account their specific characters. Indeed, these national frameworks are built with the stakeholders with the aims of protecting the users, bringing quality and distributing the offer over the whole national territory.

State Aid

In general, the pragmatic approach of the Monti-Kroes package with its aim to create more legal certainty and transparency is welcomed. Following this package, some actors are requesting from their public authorities a mandate respecting the principles of proportionality, non-discrimination, transparency in order to formalise legal security for the operators in the sector.

However, according to the replies to the consultation, there are still some clarifications to be brought and issues to be tackled and it is felt that a lot will depend on how the regulations are interpretated and applied.

First of all, regarding the clarifications, the notion of "hospital" leads to questions and it has been reported that public authorities have asked questions to the Commission in order to validate their mandates. For instance, does the notion include social welfare institutions? It has been stressed that the type of institutions covered by the notion of hospitals should be considered according to each national system. More broadly on competition rules, the notion of "undertaking" and the criteria "effect on trade" calls for clarification. The definition of an undertaking is still vague, taking into account the diversity of bodies providing social services. Although some of those bodies provide social services on payment there are other bodies that do so without payment such as voluntary organisations, foundations etc. State aid that covers only a part of their expenditures cannot be considered as "remuneration" according to the ruling on Bond van Adverteerders, since the aid does not correspond to the price value of that service. Moreover, some SSGI providers provide services in a small geographical area, e.g. in a town, or a village. The geographical coverage is so small that a question arises as to whether state aid to those bodies would satisfy the "effect on trade" criterion. This criterion is necessary for the existence of state aid according to article 87 of the Treaty.

Secondly, some issues have been highlighted regarding the requirements in the Altmark decision. Indeed, the requirement for an official act mandating the providers can be problematic in countries where the operators are autonomous. In accordance with the provisions of Community law, it is not the existence, nor the nature of the financing of the activities which induces the social general interest qualification but on the contrary the qualification which enables the public authorities to grant them public financing (direct or indirect), in particular in the form of compensation for the charges bound for the accomplishment of the mission. Even if they are entrusted with public service delegations, the social protection mutualities undertake activities of general interest of their own initiative. Moreover, there is the question of the *a priori* evaluation of the public service costs.

Regarding the required cost analysis, it is asked how to proceed when the activity is provided by only one operator or by only not-for profit providers or when there is no private company on the market to benchmark with. It has also been pointed that it is difficult to separate activities subject to competition rules from other activites, for instance, for some, the combination of obligatory and voluntary social schemes should remain possible without separate bookkeeping. Moreover, regarding the question of financing, characteristic and operational elements of the social activities have to prevail.

Therefore, it is asked to adapt the four Altmark conditions to the specificities of social services of general interest or more broadly to adapt competition rules to the specificities of social services of general interest in order to allow Member States to finance them. In this light, it is recalled that access to social services is a fundamental citizen's right and therefore the rules on government fundings should not obstruct the financing of social services. Considering that social housing and hospitals are already excluded together with small aids, some contributors propose to enlarge the exemption in the Monti-Kroes package to all social services of general interest.

Ambivalent Opinions towards EU Regulation

The outcome of the consultation is not conclusive regarding future steps at EU level. In general, most Member States and associations of local governments as well as one social partner do not see the need for a special legal instrument on social services. Most social partners for their part seem to favour a legal framework for services of general interest prior to assessing the need for further instruments for SSGI.

However indications are given on issues that could be addressed in further initiatives at EU level:

- Recognise the specific nature and role of social services and raise awareness about the essential role played by those services
- Define the characteristics of social services of general interest;
- State some principles of quality for SSGI like the evaluation of needs and participation of the beneficiaries;
- Reassess the Member States responsibility and freedom in the definition, organisation and financing of social services;
- Clarify the position of social services of general interest in regards to EU rules, notably competition, internal market and public procurement rules with the aim of balancing the specific characteristics of the sector and the current EU rules in order to promote high standards of social protection and preserve their contribution to social policy objectives;
- Define conditions for a priori compatibility with EU rules of special rights granted to providers of SSGI, of contractual or conventional relationships between providers and public authorities;
- Ensure a stable and transparent legal framework in the respect of the principle of subsidiarity as stated in the EC Treaty;

— Recognise the role played by actors from the social economy and establish at the European level the participation of social actors in the decision-making.

— Focus on cross-border situations or where exclusive rights are granted.

The principle of subsidiarity and the primary responsibility of Member States to define and organise their social services sector have been largely expressed in the contributions, by Member States but also by social partners and organisations from the civil society.

Among the Member States, only a few have expressed the advantages of a Directive on social services of general interest. For these Member States, an EU legal initiative, to be taken as soon as possible, should confirm the specific characteristics of SSGI and focus on bringing legal clarity and a stable framework which should strike the right balance between these characteristics and EU rules. This instrument should also respect Member States' freedom to organise their social services sector. For some, the scope of the Directive on SSIG would exclude social security schemes as these are non economic. Some have basically expressed their positive expectations on further legal initiatives.

The issue of finding an appropriate legal basis for such an instrument is raised. Some contributors stressed that a more detailed examination of what exactly can be achieved with which legal instrument is needed.

Six Member States do no state clearly whether they are in favour of a framework Directive on SSGI. However, they clearly express the need for more legal certainty, for instance regarding the relationship between EU rules and Member States' rights, the concept of SSGI, the need to define clear and unambiguous criteria allowing Member States to define which social services are of general interest, the need to avoid a case by case interpretation by the European Court of Justice, the need to avoid a inhomogeneous geographical implementation.

Finally many Member States have either expressed a preference for other non-legislative instruments or stressed that a legislative instrument is not necessary or appropriate for the moment, stressing that the there seems to be no added value of such a framework and that there is no evidence of any significant EU-wide problems requiring

EU-wide action, pointing out that EU-level criteria must not be applied to Member States social policy goals and highlighting that powers that belong to Member States would in this way be transferred to the European Union.

In general, organisations from the civil society welcome the idea of an EU legal initiative for social and health services of general interest aiming at providing legal certainty in the field. If needed, this Directive could be broken down into sector directives and the first of them could be a response to the recent consultation on health services It is mentioned that a piecemeal approach should be avoided to prevent conflicting approaches across different sectors of services of general interest. It is also highlighted that the scope of the directive should be on social and health services of general economic interest. In term of method, it has also been proposed to extend the pragmatic and proportional approach followed in the Monti-Kroes decision to all SSGI and to the questions relating to internal market rules and to define *a priori* conditions for compatibility with EU rules in order, on the one hand, to secure public authorities and operators and on the other hand, to allow relevant public authorities to organise and finance SSGI according to the principle of subsidiarity.

Most social partners seem to favour a legal framework for services of general interest prior to assessing the need for further instruments for SSGI. It is mentioned that instead of defining categories of services of general interest, actions should be taken to safeguard them all. Finally, some contributors are of the opinion that the principles of open competition should not be undermined. There should be full stocktaking of the delivery of social services, with no inherent bias towards public or private provision.

Exchange of Information

Monitoring coordinated by the Commission is largely welcomed by all contributors. It is also mentioned that the OMC could contribute to this specific field and the focus should be on the exchange of good practices. In this respect, topics for exchange of good practices are often mentioned: quality in the field of social services, debates on minimum standards, how to involve social partners, providers and other interested parties to find a common understanding and progress on SSGI at national level, and experience with the application of EU rules. The need for statistics and the need to define common indicators have also been stated. Some limits to the OMC are stated: the OMC would not contribute to achieving legal certainty.

However, it has been stressed that the use of the OMC in the field of social services should be limited to exchange of experiences and not go in the direction of defining common goals and indicators, nor create supplementary administrative burden for the Member States. The contributions which did not find the use of the OMC appropriate in this field also highlighted the high administrative burden.

Moreover, several contributions from social partners or organisations from the civil society stressed the necessity to involve them in the OMC in this field. Furthermore, the need for a quality initiative has been supported. Some organisations from the civil society asked for an evaluation of effectiveness and appropriateness of tendering procedures in the social sector and also for the development of some agreed quality principles for social services.

The need for the national public administrations to inform and publicise at national and local level the results and clarifications emerging at European debates on social services of general interest is recognised.

The proposed dialogue and monitoring tool in the form of biennial reports is largely welcomed and should aim at contributing to the sharing of information, including the part played by SSGI and their weight in the economy, highlighting commonalities and differences between Member States, monitoring experiences and issues arising from the application of Community rules and ECJ decisions and further develop and clarify the Community framework encompassing the SSGI. The importance of social dialogue has been stressed by many contributions from Member States, local authorities' organisations, social partners and organisations from the civil society. In general terms, the role the SPC plays in the process should be clarified and strengthened in the event of legislative proposals affecting social services.

REFERENCES

Barker, Robert L. (2003). *Social Work Dictionary* (5th ed.). Silver Spring, MD: NASW Press.

Butler, Ian and Gwenda Roberts (2004). *Social Work with Children and Families: Getting into Practice* (2nd ed.). London, England; New York, NY: Jessica Kingsley Publishers.

Sowers, Karen M. and Catherine N. Dulmus and others. (2008). *Comprehensive Handbook of Social Work and Social Welfare*. Hoboken, NJ: John Wiley & Sons.

Wittenberg, Renee (2003). *Opportunities in Social Work Careers* (Revised ed.). Chicago, IL: VGM Career Books.

6

Participation in Social Care Services

The positive contribution service users can make to social care planning and development is now recognised in government policy. Service users are taking an active role in efforts to improve both health and social care services. However, the level and extent of effective service user participation in changing and improving services is inconsistent. This can be both change and improvement in immediate services and in the culture and attitudes of the agencies and staff who deliver those services.

The remit of the Social Care Institute for Excellence (SCIE) is to develop a knowledge base for social care, so that evidence on what works best is available to everyone involved. There are many guides on how to involve service users in developing social care services, but less is known about the outcomes of that involvement.

At the beginning of this project a scoping exercise took place to see if any similar work was taking place and the reviews being commissioned by the NHS SDO were identified. SCIE did not want to duplicate this work so decided to commission work to complement these existing reviews. As a result SCIE commissioned reviews entitled 'user involvement in promoting change and enhancing the quality of services' for older people, children and young people, people with learning difficulties and disabled people.

When SCIE commissioned the reviews authors were asked to look at different types of literature. It was felt to be very important to ensure that accounts from service users that may not be published in the conventional way were included.

There was service user participation at all stages of production. A service user had equal decision-making power on the tender board that chose the successful proposals. SCIE required service users to have significant involvement in the commissioned work, and included this in the decision criteria for the tender board. In some cases service users authored the reviews. The drafts were independently assessed by people with experience as service users in the particular area under review.

The reviews drew on materials concerning user involvement in England and Wales along with relevant literature focusing on Northern Ireland and Scotland. The date range for literature and accounts was from 1992 to 2002, with seminal work before those dates included where appropriate.

Over the past 20 years several major pieces of legislation have made service user participation a requirement in many aspects of the UK health and social services. The first of these was the 1990 National Health Service and Community Care Act, which made consultation with service users a legislative duty for local authorities. Later, increased requirements for active service user participation in service development and regulation were set out in government directives on Best Value for local authorities, and the legislation associated with the New Labour public service 'modernisation' agenda.

Participation Concepts

There are long-standing debates about the distinctions to be drawn between the different types and levels of user participation. It ranges on a continuum from consultation on an individual level including feedback about services, surveys and complaints through participation in the planning and development of services to user control and management of services. Distinctions have been identified between 'consumerist' and 'democratic' approaches and agency-led and user-led initiatives, both having implications for power and control. Gradually there has been a move away from the idea of just consulting people about agency-led proposals to the notion of developing services in active partnership with those who use them; however, this is not always translated into practice.

Messages from research show the need for a range of models of involvement, depending on the level of activity that participants wish to commit. What is important is that the choice is there, and that the involvement – or partnership – is real. Further to this it has been emphasised that participation needs to be appropriate to its context and to take account of the issues involved, the objectives sought and the people who make up the target group

Service User Priorities

The social model of disability was originally conceived by the disability movement as a tool for gaining insight into their situation and to recognise how they were oppressed: It is society which disables physically impaired people. Disability is something imposed on top of our impairments. The idea that it is society that erects barriers and restricts the options and activities of disabled people has been used by others who are disempowered by social, cultural and physical structures to interpret their situations. The social model of disability has therefore become fundamental for the service user movement and the demand for independent living and citizenship rights. When service users understand participation as active citizenship it goes beyond their rights as users of social services to assert their broader rights as citizens and as people. Service users may [then] have a dual identity as consumers of services, and as citizens to whom such services are accountable.

There are clear preferences among people who use social care services for support and assistance to live independently, rather than 'care', which implies dependency. For some people, particularly older people, families and mental health service users, 'preventative' support work rather than 'crisis' intervention is seen as crucial. The service user movement has been clear about promoting the right of disadvantaged people to support and equal access to the ordinary things of life. This is consistent with the social model of disability as described above. This is reflected in what the reviews found out about the approach of service users to desired outcomes. Research has shown that older people want to help to support their independence, rather than care, and want services to be more responsive to individual preferences and changing circumstances , and that for people with learning difficulties their goals for a home, friendships, work and choices are not extraordinary, measured by the quality of life we would all expect. Similarly, for children and young people attention should be paid to the issues that children see as important, often different to the issues about which adults are most concerned. For children, day-to-day matters and issues of contact with families are of key importance.

Current Knowledge

All reviews conclude that there is a lack of research, monitoring and evaluation on the impact and outcomes of service user participation in general. Very little seems to be formally recorded at local, regional or national levels and the direct influence of user participation on transforming services has not been the subject of any major UK research studies to date.

There is some knowledge about participation techniques but little or no examination of the relationship between the process and the achievement of tangible user-led change. This is not to say that certain participation initiatives are not contributing to the improvement of services for the people who use them, but that those changes are not being properly monitored and evaluated. Monitoring impact and auditing change as a result of service user participation does not appear to be recognised as a constituent part of the whole participation process.

The literature for people with learning difficulties suggests that there seems to be a general consensus that to date it has been impossible to assess the impact of inclusive approaches to research or to planning, largely because outcomes are not always documented, or may be recorded in non-conventional ways. Within this small body of literature, knowledge of outcomes is by far the most significant gap. The reports of specific changes are haphazard and incomplete. There is currently far more documentation relating to the process than to the achievement of gains in the lives of people with learning difficulties. This may be a necessary stage and it is important to get the processes right. There is an identical situation with older people's involvement where the broad consensus emerging from researchers, inspectors and service users is that there is little evidence overall that involvement of older people is transforming services to reflect their expressed preferences and/or priorities.

For disabled people, the literature search produced a striking absence of studies evaluating the relationship between disabled user involvement in social care services and specific quality and outcomes.... Instead of using quasi-experimental research designs, the favoured approach has been to gather survey or qualitative data on the perceived impact of user involvement. This is typically in the form of ratings by service users, managers and professional providers of their satisfaction with the process and/or outcomes. In the field of participation by people who use mental health services there is a relatively weak evidence base for the impact of user involvement on organisational change.... Finally, the NHS SDO multi-sector literature review found little evidence of independent research in any of the sectors ... examined. Most of the reports were discussion papers that illustrated points raised with reference to brief case studies.

Overall, it appears that where monitoring is taking place, it is related to participation processes rather than outcomes. This suggests that some agencies may only be focusing on the intermediate aspects of how individuals experience the process, rather than combining this evaluation with that of impact and outcome. The true effectiveness of these processes to promote user-led change and impact on service improvement remains largely untested.

Intrinsic Benefits of Participation

One difficulty identified in the majority of the reviews is the tendency for agencies to focus on the 'intrinsic benefits' of participation, that is to say, how the people have gained personally from the experience of participation, rather than on the change achieved. The NHS SDO general literature review found that where participation outcomes were being monitored, this was generally in the form of qualitative process evaluation of user involvement initiatives or surveys of service users and providers involved in the process. Service user participation exercises can be an opportunity for often excluded and disenfranchised people to have a say in matters of direct concern to their lives.

Evaluation of some participation initiatives for older people have demonstrated intrinsic benefits for the users related to social contact, opportunities for learning and developments of self-esteem. There are also accounts of improved peer relations, the development of group skills, and the erosion of gender divisions between participating young people.

For mental health service users, however, the notion of 'intrinsic benefits' is sometimes translated into user participation as 'therapy', an understanding that is thought to have negative consequences: there is an argument to be made that some 'supportive' professional attitudes can limit the impact and effectiveness by reducing this to individual therapeutic outcomes. That is, user involvement may be endorsed by professionals as performing a therapeutic or rehabilitative function in enhancing individuals' skills, competence and self-esteem. However, it is also noted that the purpose of self-advocacy is to produce change and that involvement must be about a collective voice for people with learning difficulties, not just about individuals.... Often, when self-advocates speak up and participate, it is not only for the intermediate individual benefits, but to demand service change.

It has been argued that the success of user involvement projects cannot be measured solely by reference to objective changes with service agencies. However, findings emerging from the reviews suggest that while individual experiences are being monitored in some cases, objective changes to service quality remain unmeasured. If the reason for consulting disabled people is not clearly thought through then the form of consultation becomes more important than the content or outcome. While attention may be paid to the quality of the process for the individual, outcomes and change as a result of participation may not be realised.

Individual service user experience of participation mechanisms should be monitored, so that agencies can learn from both positive and negative responses and improve the process. User research in the voluntary sector has shown that by frequently asking themselves and others what worked well and why, users and managers developed systems of continuous feedback, which enabled them to learn, and adapt. The reviews positively indicate that it is important to monitor both process and outcome, and note that the success of participation should not be reduced to individual at the expense of organisational outcomes. Agencies are advised against satisfaction with 'intrinsic benefits' alone, but should respond to what service users have said during the participation process.

Feedback

The reviews show that service users require feedback about the impact of their participation. Service users say they need not only to feel the changes in their lives as a result of improvement at individual or service level, but also need to receive feedback as an integral part of the participation process. The Audit Commission has stressed the importance of change beginning and ending with users or consumers. Emerging findings show that agencies should see monitoring of impact and meaningful feedback as a vital constituent of the user participation initiative, as it is related to engagement and commitment.

The NHS SDO general literature review on user participation in managing change reports there is general agreement that in order to achieve sustained involvement of users it is important to provide adequate time and resources to make their contribution and to ensure that those taking part receive feedback on how their contribution affected service delivery. Emphasis in the literature on process, rather than outcomes, of user involvement suggests that users often do not have the information to judge whether their participation made a difference.

This situation is common to many service users and has led to criticism from different groups of people. For example, the self-advocacy movement of people with learning difficulties has a very action-oriented approach. Self-advocacy should be about action – ie how to achieve real and long-lasting change. When the action taken as a result of participation is not communicated, self-advocates often report dissatisfaction and frustration. Children are helped by being clear about the process of decision making, about the reason for their involvement and where their opinions will go, what will be done with them, and how and when they will receive feedback. Disabled people too report that there is a further risk of 'involvement fatigue' with too many consultation initiatives that have little impact on service standards or profiles.

Participation and Change at An Individual Level

At individual 'consumer' level, community care legislation has given adult service users the right to involvement in constructing their own care or support packages, the idea being to provide choice and greater flexibility to the consumer. Legislation concerning services for children and young people says that they should have the opportunity to voice their preferences. Research from the learning difficulties field has shown that individual life changes can create a groundswell for change, and so methodologies such as person-centred planning and Direct Payments that will help individuals and families move forward are very important. Some of the SCIE commissioned reviews looked at the individual service aspects of participation in change, in the context of the wider participation agenda.

Choice and Control

So far evidence in this area is patchy but inspection reports, qualitative studies and accounts from service users suggest that exercise of choice as an individual 'welfare consumer' remains restricted, particularly if you are from a black or minority ethnic group or are lesbian or gay.

There still appears to be a lack of opportunity for people to have a say in their own services. As regards the exercise of choice for older people, service users report that they feel 'consulted' rather than 'involved' and for some there was a sense of powerlessness in what to them was a complex or confusing system. Research also indicated that users were restricting their choices at assessment because of a perception that local authorities had limited resources for community care. For black and minority ethnic older people, research shows that there is still poor communication and availability of information about available services as well as indication that minority ethnic older people are less likely to find an appropriate care provider.

The participation of children and young people in their individual care planning also has identified limitations. The report emphasises that it is a cause for concern that a wide range of studies report that children continue to feel that they are not listened to despite a statutory framework for participation.... Children perceive these meetings as boring, repetitive, intrusive and also frightening. It is noted that the processes to allow children and young people to exercise choice may not be working well for those who are younger, from a minority ethnic background, disabled or looked after.

For children and young people and people with learning difficulties, the ability to make choices was often limited by a lack of information about options and preparatory information for meetings, along with a lack of support or creative communication in decision making. The review for people with learning difficulties notes that service users as consumers can be pervasively marginalised by lack of knowledge about their own situation , knowledge vital for enabling choice and control. Disabled people have found that assessment of eligibility for services can pose difficulties for exercising choice and control. Decisions about access to assessments are often influenced by service criteria based on risk and budgetary concerns. There is evidence that there can be potential for improvement if users are involved in developing assessment and care management forms. Research also points to the importance of creatively engaging service users in the continual consultation and review of how the care or support is working for them, not just at initial assessment stage.

Direct Payments

Through the collective campaigning efforts of service users and their allies, Direct Payments were introduced in 1996. Disabled people, people with learning difficulties, mental health service users and now older people are entitled to use local authority funds to purchase their own personal assistance. Although there is a general agreement among service users that Direct Payments are a very positive development, their implementation by local authorities and the extent to which they are publicised remains inconsistent.

The review for disabled people showed that the provision is uneven geographically with, for example, disproportionately more personal assistant users in South East England. Many local authorities have been extremely reluctant to introduce Direct Payments, while some within the disabled community have found it difficult to access payment schemes. There are recurring obstacles that include a lack of appropriate information and awareness among professionals, and a lack of peer support. For older people professional 'know best' attitudes can be a barrier, as illustrated by assumptions made by agencies about people's interest in taking up Direct Payments. Without appropriate support, older people have reported feeling more like supplicants than purchasers when dealing with service providers.

There are similar issues for people with learning difficulties and the NHS SDO review notes that the degree of support that users receive in recruiting and employing personal care can impact heavily on the 'success' of these schemes from the perspective of users, as well as on the conditions of employment experienced by employed workers.

Although Direct Payments give people greater flexibility and choice about who provides their individual assistance, the review noted that homecare is provided by imperfect local markets currently characterised by lack of information for both users and workers , a situation which can impede exercise of choice for both concerned. In some cases the limited choice has led to the establishment of user-controlled service providers and services by and for black and minority ethnic people. Evaluation of user-led organisations for disabled people has shown that there was overwhelming agreement that user-led organisations were far more responsive to disabled people's support needs both in terms of what was on offer and how it was delivered, with peer support a major consideration. However, the issue of regional inconsistency extends to the availability of user-controlled services for disabled people, with the majority clustered in South East England.

Complaints

Local authorities have formal complaints procedures intended to enable individuals to exercise some control over the quality of services. The intention is to increase accountability, improve customer relations, promote quality assurance and prevent conflict or litigation. Potentially the data from the complaints feedback mechanism could be used as an indicator of service quality and possible areas for change and improvement.

The findings for children, young people and their families were clearest. The review states that although all local authorities have complaints procedures there is evidence that a sizeable proportion of children are unaware of their existence ... [research indicates] that there are long delays in dealing with complaints, that attempts to resolve complaints informally can inhibit access to the formal procedures, and that there is a continuing need for staff training and support to ensure that the procedures operate fairly and efficiently. In addition, parents as advocates for children fear that complaints to children's services may put children at risk of retaliation. There are similar issues for older people as elderly people in residential care [can be] reluctant and ill-informed 'consumers', easily intimidated by fear of those they may wish to complain of.

The NHS SDO general review of literature on this topic showed that for service users wanting to change or improve services, complaints procedures may not work effectively. This can be because of the disparity in status between complainants and the professionals they complain of, which may be exacerbated in contexts where users are 'coerced' into 'using' services. In reality, departments may not publicise their procedures adequately, given the range of vulnerable, sensorily impaired and non-English speakers they provide services to. People may be reluctant to use the complaints system because they are concerned about possible repercussions or fear loss of services.

Organisational Commitment and Responsiveness

Despite the overall lack of research or recorded knowledge illuminating the relationship between user participation and service change and improvement, the reviews show strong indications of why change may not be occurring. Organisational responsiveness was an issue common to all the reviews. What do agencies and services do with the reported needs, recommendations and action points generated through participation exercises? Are they acted upon? Although the findings from the reviews suggest there is little evidence about whether action is taking place as a result of user involvement, general and specific barriers to change can be identified.

The NHS SDO literature review reports that frequently cited barriers to successful user involvement include professional and organisational resistance. For mental health service users, the review suggests that the role of organisational culture is key in both facilitating or impeding user/carer involvement in change management. The situation is similar for children and young people as the evidence from the few evaluations that exist suggests that the participation of children and young people is having little impact on decisions made in relation to agency policy and practice.

Similarly, for older people the review indicates that the main barriers for service users in affecting change in services relate to how ready social and health care agencies are to respond to the increasingly clear messages from users about the type of services that are important to them and the way they are delivered. The review for older people gives further emphasis to the importance of commitment: the issue, in terms of achieving change seems to be less one of finding effective ways of engaging older people, than that of a commitment to responding to the views so clearly expressed by older service users.

The findings indicate that a fundamental political commitment to change should be driving the participation agenda. The intention to change as a result of user participation should be established prior to its implementation. The Audit Commission emphasises this: consultation should relate clearly to a decision that the authority plans to make, and is open to influence. It should be made clear 'what consultees can change by responding to the consultation'. For children and young people the point made in the literature that even though training and other events might be very good, they are unlikely to make a difference if the political will for participation is lacking. The review for the participation of disabled people directs these key questions at those developing and planning services: how committed are you? What are your main reasons for involving people?… Are you prepared to act on what they tell you? How will you deal with the change in the balance of power that meaningful involvement brings?.

Power Relations

The principal barriers identified in the literature are the power differentials and dynamics between service users and professionals. Power issues underlie the majority of identified difficulties with effective user-led change. The message is that any user participation initiative requires continual awareness of the context of power relations in which it is being conducted. These power relations are historical and can pervade at both systemic and individual levels. The traditional division between service user and professional is rooted in history of 'welfare' in the UK. Historically, people who use social services were seen as passive recipients of charity and care. Decision-making power about that care traditionally lay in the hands of the providers, as did the opportunity to assert expertise. This situation has been challenged and eroded through the efforts of service users and their allies. Recent legislation has marked a theoretical movement away from paternalistic to partnership-based approaches.

The NHS SDO general literature review on user involvement in change revealed various problems with systems and power: employee respondents to a survey of local authorities suggested that 'administrative systems are designed to support institutions rather than people'.... Other difficulties, shared by other sectors, include lack of clarity about how far managers 'were really prepared to go along the consultation – participation – power sharing continuum'. Others pointed out the dangers of grafting 'token' users or carers onto existing planning and operational structures ... either the user and carer become institutionalised, or both sides continue to have very different agendas. It is also emphasised that professionals still exercise considerable power over disabled people's lives. Each profession assumes a language, a set of values and practices that privileges the practitioner. Hitherto, a clear division between the expert provider and lay user has reinforced their enhanced status.

Specific problems with power sharing are further highlighted in the reviews, including notions of expertise, dominant professional perspectives and attitudes towards service user decision-making capability. Generally, the NHS SDO report identified professional power, assumptions about expert knowledge, professional defensiveness and lack of organisational expertise in engaging with service users as impeding the process of change. Similarly, resistant organisation or professional cultures and embedded power differentials are seen as primary obstacles to user involvement in formal representative structures for mental health service users. For children and young people constructive and ongoing involvement in decision making is more likely in organisations which have developed a participatory culture: one in which children are encouraged to participate in small as well as big decisions. Empowering children in this way may require adults to rethink how they share their power. Their demands must be offset against those of other (including more powerful) stakeholders. Managers retain power at the centre of a network mediating the competing interests of professionals, users, carers, the public and political actors. A shift from top-down hierarchies to more inclusive networks or markets in the organisation of public services in these ways can produce new techniques for legitimising managerial and professional power.

The reviews show that the relative values placed on different types of expertise and language and the professional assumptions about decision-making competence can make it difficult for users to be heard, or to make an impact on decisions. Users of health and social care services frequently complain of the unreasonable expectation that they present their views in managerial language: failing to do so may mean those views are never considered seriously. There remains the need for a move towards recognising the validity and respecting the worth of the unique expertise that service users have developed through experience. Some mental health service users now favour the term 'experts by experience'. A passage from the review for people with learning difficulties exemplifies the general situation: people with learning difficulties come to the table so that they can bring 'lived experience' of themselves and those they represent. It is emphasised that people with learning difficulties who get involved with changes can vastly improve the process because they can ground the decisions in their own lived experience.

Specific issues about the language of expertise are detailed in the review for disabled people: a further problem for professionals is that their claim to expertise and self-regulation does not sit easily with user participation. Likewise, the value placed on experiential knowledge and the language for its expression has also been an issue for people who use mental health services: the experiential knowledge of users may be valued for its authenticity but when set beside knowledges which can claim status of 'evidence' that authenticity occupies second place. In addition, the direct experience of users and the way it is expressed may sometimes be dismissed as too distressing or disturbing. Research from the voluntary sector indicates that good quality, two-way communication between users and decision makers benefited users and promoted change in organisations. An emphasis on dialogue highlighted that the views of both parties were equally valid.

Difficulties with professional ideas of 'competency' or decision-making ability/ responsibility are indicated in the reviews for people with learning difficulties, children and young people and mental health service users. For those involved in mental health services, user involvement is pervaded by ambivalence. On the one hand the experience of services is seen as a direct and authentic expression of what is acceptable and what is not. On the other, being mentally ill is itself seen to disrupt the possibility of rational action. The general indications are that in all areas of involvement, 'information giving and consultation were most common, and only very rarely are users and carers given full decision-making power'. But for people with learning difficulties, and others, the ability to participate fully in decision making is often determined by circumstances rather than 'competence': people with learning difficulties often report that they are controlled by their own service staff; their power to be influential in change is limited by. With regard to the role of the supporter in user participation initiatives, self-advocates have recommended that supporters need to break from the service tradition, in which people with learning disabilities are usually engulfed, and assist people in overturning the power balance. With children and young people there can be a degree of professional anxiety about sharing power and responsibility: adults should recognise that encouraging participation does not mean handing over responsibility for decision making to children.

Despite some professional misgivings about user expertise and decision-making ability, it is also reported that service users who are assertive and articulate may be seen as 'unrepresentative' and therefore at risk of being ignored. It appears to be a particular problem that users and carers are asked to be more 'representative' than any other group of stakeholders in the change management process. Articulate users may be criticised as unrepresentative because 'ordinary' users are often not seen as articulate. Service users who articulate the need for changes that agencies may not be willing or able to implement have sometimes been labelled as 'unrepresentative': implementing changes suggested by service users that are cost neutral and make services more efficient is a relatively simple task. Implementing changes that require reallocation of resources becomes more difficult, especially if these conflict with nationally defined service priorities. In such instances the validity of user views or the representativeness of service users who participate may be questioned. Concern about achieving 'representativeness' is identified in most of the reviews.

An enhanced social and political understanding of the user movement among professionals may improve understanding of service user representation issues. It is also noted that the active involvement of older people in enabling others to have a say is another trend and represents a move away from the tendency reporting in earlier reviews of speaking 'for' older people. Many service user controlled organisations and advocacy schemes have innovative approaches to participation, and have a distinctive role in empowering users to collectively take action. Issues of inclusion and representation should be addressed with service users. It appears that agencies have a responsibility, in collaboration with users, to undertake checks about how strategies resulting from user involvement match the expectations and wishes of all service users.

Partnership or Consultancy

There is some indication in the review findings that user participation initiatives can become consultation exercises to approve of service planning and policy proposals, rather than enabling service users to be key players or partners in their formulation. The reviews show that many organisations have an understanding of participation that still positions service users as external consultants rather than partners in the development process. In the social care field, local authorities and agencies tend to use one-off consultation processes generally in order to comply with the requirement to consult users as part of an initiative directed by central government.... Less common is the sort of activity designed to enable children and young people to have an ongoing involvement in the work of the agency. Mental health service users report that models of change management generally position service users as external stakeholders , suggesting that they often remain outside the central sphere of influence and decision making. However, the research suggests that embedded participation based on a partnership approach could be most effective at achieving lasting change. There have to be structures for continuing to work together and to hear the voice of people who use services. Generally, the reviews reveal there is a danger that government demands for agencies to demonstrate user involvement may mean that user activities become a formal procedure to be ticked off rather than an embedded and powerful organisational practice.

The work on disabled people and mental health service users highlights an emerging trend termed 'the technology of legitimation', in which managers seek user approval for their decisions: some critics argue that user involvement is too easily exploited as a 'technology of legitimation'. Thus, it sustains management and government authority by giving the appearance of democratising public services without allowing policy shifts in 'undesirable' directions. Indeed, managers and professionals are both prone to 'play the user card' in trying to win a policy dispute. Strategies of user involvement can work to reinforce the power of professionals and managers. Indications of such legitimating activity have also been found for children and young people: forums, the method used most commonly by local authorities, are least popular with young people and not something they suggest. Significant problems have been identified with this type of activity: often they lack a sense of purpose, are not well integrated with local decision making structures, are not accountable to other young people in the area, and are seen as a token group of young people used to legitimise adult decisions.

Some discussion has centred on the role of participation 'champions' or leaders in promoting cultural change and organisational commitment. While it has been asserted that user involvement requires 'champions' throughout the organisation for it to flourish , the role of professional allies remains under-explored. There are concerns that agencies may rely solely on the commitment of one individual rather than embedding participation in organisational practice, and that individual managers may only be interested in the role for career advancement. On the other hand, some user authors take a more positive approach to those professionals whom they perceive to have helped sustain the momentum of a user group.

Research suggests that embedded, continuous but varied participation approaches that engage service users in decision making have most potential for influencing change. The majority of service users wish to represent themselves directly, collectively or through a peer advocate in decision-making forums. The less favoured approach is having input mediated through external consultation exercises and questionnaires that could be vulnerable to different professional interpretations. Service users should be understood as active partners, albeit in an often unequal partnership.

Finally, agencies are recommended to re-examine their notion of service users who are thought to be 'hard to reach'. Some service users may lack structures of representation; may find it difficult to meet with [other] service users and managers; or may be hampered by attitudinal and legislative deficiencies that fail to promote their rights to involvement. Paradoxically, it is indicated that for some service users those who remain excluded from participation processes may be those who make higher use of services. For older people with dementia, this has prompted the recommendation for consultation to become an integral part of ongoing individual care.

Conflict and Expectations

Biehal discusses consultation with users as an aid to greater managerial efficiency, but warns that 'this will not necessarily be accompanied by any real increase in the power of service users to determine the range and quality of the services available to them'. Discrepancy between what managers want of user involvement and what users want may be a major source of dissatisfaction for service users. Some reviews note that dissatisfaction and even conflict may be an inevitable part of the user participation process. Self-advocates assert that for people with learning difficulties speaking up is not just about having polite interactions around the table and the most clear-cut examples of self-advocacy led initiatives are local and reactive: they are protests made against decisions by others. Mental health service users' experience of the participation process has shown that it is a mistake to assert that conflicts should or can be resolved before the process of change is begun.

At the front-line level there can be tension between workers and users/carers. Managers and other staff may see user involvement as both of value and a threat. One way of understanding this is as a conflict between staff and managers' desire to implement a rather limited consumerist agenda and the hunger of many users to reclaim their spoiled identity and reassert themselves as citizens.

User involvement in change management will work best when front-line staff and other stakeholders are also meaningfully engaged in organisational processes. However, conflicts will inevitably arise between the various actors. Again, people with learning difficulties have found that the engagement of front-line staff in user participation is needed, but there can be a disparity between policy makers, management and front-line staff: one of the main points ... was about the importance of staff in services, particularly in day services. The research suggests that front-line practitioners who have most contact with service users could be usefully engaged in user participation strategies and benefit from user-led training focusing on the practice and principles of user participation. The motivation and commitment of front-line practitioners can also be compromised by organisational structures and audit cultures. Organisations and their managers should support front-line practitioners to focus on user concerns, as they may be inhibited from doing so by unhelpful processes or timetables. Research has shown that user-centred activity within the voluntary sector was promoted where leaders: created space for users and staff to debate user involvement and to develop and try out ideas [and] encouraged and supported users and staff.

Limited financial and other resources along with conflicting priorities emerge from the reviews as restraints on the degree to which service users may be able to influence changes in services. There may be restrictions on the ability of an organisation to respond positively, including its service remit. User research has shown that the need for a holistic approach to support: other services were very important to people beyond ideas of social care, in particular housing and information. Lack of honest information can create confusion and disillusionment as well as preventing meaningful engagement and change. Similarly, service users should be empowered to voice their limits and expectations. These approaches could go some way to preventing unnecessary conflict during the process.

Mismatches in timing, participation and meeting methods and expectations, financial constraints and coordination difficulties all arose, with planning groups unable to meet tight timetables effectively marginalised despite the effort expended by participants. Control and power remains with practitioner/ managers, whose guiding principles may be financial. Professionals may sometimes comment on unreasonable expectations of users who choose not to consider financial restraints and imperatives, while it may be that users are not permitted to consider them. For disabled people user involvement has increased over recent years. While this has been welcomed by disabled people and their organisations, it has also exposed the limitations of the rhetoric of empowerment within a 'social care' environment that is subject to tight budgetary controls. Managers have relative operational autonomy but only within strict budgetary controls and performance targets. In such an organisational environment there is far less opportunity for partnership with disabled people … user-led agendas [risk being] overtaken by a contrary set of political and economic constraints.

Development of mutual understanding, effective communication and conflict resolution takes time but review findings show that the pace of work itself can be exclusionary and could potentially affect the quality of engagement with service users. People who have been excluded need to be able to trust the people they are working with, to know that other people will take them seriously and will do what they say they are going to do. Self-advocates feel strongly that the process of change needs to slow down, and to be more thorough, so that involvement does not become tokenistic , while research for older people points to the importance of allowing time and space for effective participation, particularly for more marginalised older people such as those who are frail and housebound or have dementia. Disabled people's evaluation of participation processes identified the fact that there was too little time for meaningful discussion. Deadlines for completing tasks can also be drawn too tightly to be realistic. The resourcing and core funding of user participation and user groups was explored by several reviews. The findings point to the importance of supporting user groups to maintain their independence and critical function: some measure of independent and critical thinking is necessary to make changes happen at a fundamental level, so that involvement does not simply mean collusion. The provision of specific budgets for user participation has also been identified as a potential change enabler, with the allocation of money also demonstrating a tangible commitment beyond its practical use. Again, resourcing appears ultimately to be a power sharing issue.

Diversity and Marginalisation

The reviews showed that attention to the diversity of service users in terms of race, culture, sexuality and, in some cases, disability was lacking in mainstream services and participation initiatives. This relates to both diversity within user groups and the relative lack of knowledge about user participation for marginalised people. The majority of research identified in the reviews concerned issues for black and minority ethnic people.

It has already been established that at the level of individual service provision, the needs of black and minority ethnic people and those who identify as lesbian or gay are not being adequately addressed. This has, in some cases, resulted in the development of particular user-led service providers aiming to meet those needs: users who feel marginalised or inadequately provided for by mainstream or statutory services may move towards establishing voluntary sector services, aiming to provide mutual support and advocacy against discriminatory practices and institutions. Consistent with this, the review of Social Services Inspectorate reports revealed that much of the service provision for black and minority ethnic older people is in the voluntary sector.

The challenge to mainstream services is to creatively engage marginalised peoples, the concerns of whom often extend beyond service provision to creating positive social and political identities in the face of discrimination: Black and minority ethnic groups may have difficulty in subordinating their objectives to the narrow [services] agenda, and may be unwilling to act as collaborators … it [has been] argued that for some people previous attempts to influence health and social care services have proved so unsatisfactory that separation is less demoralising. There are fewer efforts to investigate service needs than to engage with 'the community' or the 'power brokers' in the community, in more superficial ways. Black and minority ethnic elders have reported feeling over-researched; they wanted to see some effective action and to become involved in decisions that affected them. In addition, service users may also be stereotyped according to the expectations of service providers , such as the myth of extended families providing care for older and disabled relatives.

As regards the participation of people with learning difficulties one of the big challenges is to hear the voices of all those who are supposedly represented by [the] process, including those from black and minority ethnic communities and people with high support needs. For older people, while there are pockets of good practice, the overall impression is that basic communication with minority ethnic groups is still at a rudimentary stage ; our analysis endorses the points made by other research reviews that there is a need for better understanding of issues relating to exploring and supporting the involvement of: older gay and lesbian people; people living with long-term conditions and disabilities; black and minority ethnic older people; people in rural areas. The situation is very similar for children and young people as well as disabled people and mental health service users: structural and cultural barriers contribute to an under-representation of some groups among disabled users. There is evidence that alternative methods, as opposed to formal processes, of consulting children are rarely used, indicating possibly a lack of sufficient staff with the skills to communicate with children, particularly young children and disabled children.

The reviews show that marginalisation from both appropriate services and participation processes does not only occur because of race, culture and sexuality. Living in rural or certain geographical areas can have a bearing on exclusion from structures for participation. The very young and the very old, particularly those with dementia, the homeless and travellers, people in institutional or residential care, people with addiction problems and those with severe disabilities and high support needs or needs that cut across traditional service categories seldom have the opportunity to be heard or to influence service change. It is also recommended that poverty should be considered as an important overarching issue. And when they do know, they are often denied the opportunity to exercise it because of a lack of resources, support, education, self-confidence or the respect of others.

A key message from the review for children and young people could also apply to other people who are often excluded from the participation process: little is known about why young people choose not to be involved, or why they get excluded ... of relevance there is the definition of use of the term 'hard to reach'. There is a danger in seeing this as something to do with the children and young people themselves rather than a reflection of an agency's ability to communicate with a wide range of children and families. Increased awareness is recommended: in addition to promoting organisational cultures that are conducive to user involvement in general, arguments also arise in this field about the need for cultural sensitivity on the part of professionals and organisations in relation to different user needs, as is the need for adequate resourcing: the expansion of ... self-advocacy groups, and the 'mainstreaming' of minority issues in wider ... services, will be constrained by lack of resources unless a commitment to minority ethnic needs can be built into the contract culture in health and social services.

Messages from the Research for Policy Makers

This overview suggests that efforts to involve people in the planning and development of the services they use are taking place across the UK. What remains unclear is the impact of that participation. At local and regional levels policy makers would be advised to integrate change mapping and feedback into the whole participation process. Monitoring and evaluation techniques should be developed with service users. At national level a programe of research addressing the outcomes, at different levels, of different approaches to user involvement could be instigated and developed in partnership with service users. The research in this overview points to a transition from this first, adaptive stage to a second stage of transformational change. This means looking at how organisations can transform in response to service user participation, now the principle has been established.

Professionals now need to interact with service users as partners in strategic planning arenas as well as at front-line service delivery level. As a result the stereotyped ideas about service users, dominant professional perspectives on expertise and the language for its expression, conflicting priorities and power dynamics are among the factors that may be impeding progress. It appears that involving front-line staff in participation strategies and providing user-led awareness training could help improve user/ professional relations at both strategic and service delivery level. Supported, open and respectful communication is key.

Challenges to traditional professional modes of thinking and operating are emerging as a result of participation. The reviews indicate that organisational culture and structure also needs to respond and change in order to accommodate new partnerships and new ways of working with people who have often been oppressed and marginalised. Organisations require policies and procedures that engender positive political commitment and minimise resistance to user-led change. User-led research could usefully reveal more about the role of professional allies in promoting change.

The issue of power sharing needs to be openly discussed at every level so that users and professionals have the opportunity to share experiences, explore the meaning of partnership and independence and develop new structures and approaches to service, and indeed organisational development. The desire of service users for holistic approaches to support and assistance seems to have influenced their approaches to participation. The political and philosophical methods of the service user movement seem to be exposing the limitations of traditional, fragmented service categories for organising participation designed to promote strategic change. Participation provides a unique opportunity for organisations to develop and transform through critical enquiry with service users using the social model of disability, ideas about control, oppression, rights, poverty and citizenship.

References

Axinn, June and Mark J. Stern (2008). *Social Welfare: A History of the American Response to Need* (7th ed.). Boston, MA: Pearson/Allyn and Bacon.

Balgopal, Pallassana R. (2000). *Social Work Practice with Immigrants and Refugees*. New York, NY: Columbia University Press.

Barker, Richard (2009). *Making Sense of Every Child Matters - multi professional practice guidance* (1st ed.). Bristol, UK: Policy Press.

7

Social Work and Human Rights

The International Federation of Social Workers (IFSW) and the International Association of Schools of Social Work (IASSW) consider it imperative that those involved in the field of social work education and practice have a clear and unreserved commitment to the promotion and protection of human rights and to the satisfaction of fundamental social aspirations.

IFSW and IASSW believe that greater knowledge and understanding of human rights will improve the actions and interventions of social work professionals for the benefit of those who require their services.

Social workers work with their clients on a variety of levels: the micro level of individual and family; the meso level of community; and the macro level of society—nationally and internationally.

Schools of social work are strongly encouraged to develop creative ways of incorporating human rights content into their curricula. Some schools may offer a separate elective course, some may require students to pursue a course on human rights, and others may integrate human rights content into all their required foundation courses. A separate human rights course provides the opportunity to study the issues in depth as they apply to social work. If the course is an elective one, hovever, only the students who choose to take the course are reached. Infusing the content into all foundation courses has the advantage of reaching all students, as would a required course;

However the human rights curriculum materials are used, it is essential that the philosophy, the teaching and the structure of the educational process, as well as the content, reflect the human rights and so:ial justice dimensions. Four broad areas require attention with regard to the learning process. First, the philcsophy and mission of the schools need to be explicit and must be seen to permeate and inspire the learning process. Secondly, the structure of the schools must reflect human rights concerns in terms of policies, procedures and organisational factors relating to admissions advising, grading and evaluation of students, on the one hand, and issues affecting faculty, such as hiring practices, assessments and promotions, on the other. The third area is that of faculty-student relations. Creating an open environment is important in the classroom and in developing a sense of equality among students and between students and faculty. In short, if one is to teach about human rights, one must respect and uphold students' rights. A fourth area for attention concerns the social work practice methods being taught in the classroom. If one is to engender a commitment to human rights, the methods by which social work is taught must themselves uphold human rights.

Conceptual Development of Human Rights

The historical development of the current concept of human rights is often traced from the eighteenth century, culminating in the American Declaration of Independence and the French Declaration of the Rights of Man. It is important, however, to recognise that many of the core elements of human rights were present and enforced in western and non-western cultures and societies from ancient times.

The development of human rights has been one of evolution. A concern for civil and political rights, which was the initial spur to the conceptualisation of human rights in the eighteenth century, was gradually matched by a demand for economic, social and cultural rights. Now a third generation of rights is increasingly recognised as a legitimate universal aspiration for humankind—rights to peace, development and a clean environment protected from destruction.

Economic, social and cultural rights progressed more slowly than civil and political rights. The extension of participation in democratic structures through suffrage, first to members of the middle and working classes, and subsequently to women, was seen as the expression of rights which would now be termed "civil and political".

The consequences of the Industrial Revolution first drew the attention of social reformers.

Initially, that response was influenced by philanthropy and individual charity. The development of any acknowledgement of collective responsibility for social ills followed those initiatives and took the form of transfer payments with the evolution of insurance schemes. Yet while the first signs of a collective responsibility can be seen in legislative developments in Western Europe in the late nineteenth century, at the same time Western Europe was extending its colonial grip on the West Indies, Asia and Africa. The impact of colonialism has been well documented.

The development of an organised concept of social welfare came as social activists recognised the inadequacy of an individual response to a collective problem. Social workers began to join together, to share ideas and experience, to develop their practice, and to express a collective response to the issues they encountered. There was a shared desire to condemn warfare and to develop an institutional framework for international cooperation.

The establishment of the League of Nations and the International Labour Organisation and treinception of social welfare organisations such as the International Conference of Social Welfare, the International Committee of Schools of Social Work and the International Permanent Secretariat of Social Workers in the 1920s were evidence of this new mood of international, regional and national collaboration. Social work organisations focused their attention on the establishment of the profession and its value base in individual countries.

Ironically, it was another global conflict—the Second World War—which was to be the stimulus for the next great stage of development in human rights. The Second World War led countries throughout tie world to adopt a new framework for international CDoperation. There was a recognition that norms of intenational behaviour needed to be expressed as rights.

Such new frameworks for international cooperation also had their impact on social work organisations, nationally and internationally A global solidarity began to emerge in the profession's vision. Social work organisations grew in number, scope and geographical array across the world.

Philosophical Values

The values identified in this section, though illustrative rather than exhaustive, are central to the role of social workers and schools of social work in pressing for values education at all levels in society, and in training for professionals. The values also underpin the human rights dimension in training for social workers and others. Many of the problems encountered by social workers at the micro, meso and macro levels in different spheres stem from an underlying crisis of values.

Life

Value for life is a sine qua non for all human rights work. The worth of life, human and non-human existence, is the fountain-head for all other ideals and values that follow. This implies not only opposing the negation of life, but also positive and affirming aspects. Wherever possible, the profession has not only to resist violations of human rights, but actively to support all life-promoting and nurturing activities. This is so that there can be fulfilment of human existence. Life is intrinsically connected and interdependent in all its parts and forms, human and non-human. Disruption of any of its aspects affects the social fabric or thread of life, thereby injuring humankind. Value of life implies that suffering and death are not just individual phenomena; they touch others just as joy, happiness and life do.

Physical health is an important aspect of the value and quality of life.

In many countries social workers have to work with clients affected environmental factors. They are also confronted with serious dilemmas in their practice relating to matters such as contraception, abortion, or their clients' management of terminal illness. The value and quality of life will be among the considerations which can assist them in their counselling activities.

Freedom And Liberty

The principle that "all human beings are born free" is contained in the first two articles of the Universal Declaration of Human Rights. The fundamental freedoms—the right to liberty; freedom from slavery and servitude; freedom from torture and cruel, inhuman or degrading treatment or punishment; freedom from arbitrary arrest, detention or exile; freedom from arbitrary interference with privacy, family, home or correspondence; and freedom of movement and residence.

To be born free and having the right to liberty presupposes that each human being has the freedom of choice in the conduct of his or her life. The enjoyment of this freedom is, however, frequently curtailed by material and other constraints. Freedom is likewise restricted by the principle of not infringing the freedom of others. Yet freedom, next to life itself, is viewed as the most precious human value, closely linked to human dignity and to the worth of human life. The quest for freedom and liberty has inspired many peoples to seek release from territorial or geographical domination. The quest for spiritual and intellectual freedom has inspired heroic acts of resistance. At a personal level, freedom from one's own emotions can be conducive to peace and harmony.

Equality and Non-discrimination

The fundamental principle of equality for all human beings is set out in article 1 of the Universal Declaration of Human Rights. It is, however, imperfectly applied in everyday life, not least in the manifold aspects of interpersonal relations. For social workers it is a crucial concept for personal and professional attitudes.

Once the principle of equality is accepted, it becomes impossible to discriminate against any person or group of persons. Non-discrimination is, in fact, based on the twin principles of equality and dignity. Discrimination can reduce a human being to a function, a quality, an opinion, whereby a person is no longer perceived in his or her unique diversity and wholeness.

Discrimination can be said to be the denial of the fundamental and universally accepted rights of all human beings to persons or groups of person who are excluded. Discrimination takes various forms. The grounds for discrimination set out in all relevant international instruments: "without distinction of any kind, such as race, colour, sex, language, religion, political or other opinion, national or social origin, property, birth or other status" are not exhaustive. New grounds for discrimination appear constantly in a changing world as additional freedoms are recognised, problems arise, and technological and other developments create changes in life-styles and working traditions.

JUSTICE

Various aspects of justice have to be taken into consideration: the legal, judicial, social, economic and other aspects which constitute the basis of a society up-holding the dignity of its members, and ensuring security and integrity of persons. In its international instruments, the United Nations has provided valuable principles and binding commitments against, inter alia, arbitrary deprivation of freedom and interference with privacy, and for protection under the law. In cases of violations of the law, persons are to be assured of a prompt and fair trial by an objective judicial authority. If found guilty, they should be entitled to humane treatment whose purpose is the reform and social integration of the individual.

Social workers have long promoted such principles and are conscious of the fact that human rights are best upheld by a law-abiding State. But the pursuit of justice also has wider implications, less easily codified. Social justice encompasses satisfaction of basic human needs and the equitable sharing of material resources. It aims at universal access to fundamental services in the areas of health and education, equal opportunities at the start, protection for disadvantaged persons or groups, and a degree of moderation in the areas of retribution, consumption and profit.

SOLIDARITY

Solidarity is another fundamental intrinsic value which implies not only understanding and empathy towards humankind's pain and suffering, but also identifying and taking a stand with the sufferers and their cause. Social workers are expected not only to stand by people who are struggling, but also to express their solidarity in words and deeds in the face of any form of denial of people's political, civil, social, economic, cultural or spiritual rights.

Solidarity can likewise be extended in natural disasters, and is essential in the many tragedies arising from want, inequitable distribution of resources, social neglect and injustice. Poverty, hunger, starvation, homelessness and denial of the means of subsistence are perhaps some of the greatest violations of human rights that are not sufficiently recognised. In the final analysis, it is the firm stand of social workers and many others with sufferers and victims of human rights violations that can make a difference by strengthening the sufferers' resolve and relieving their isolation.

SOCIAL RESPONSIBILITY

Social responsibility is action undertaken on behalf of sufferers and victims: standing for them, championing their cause and helping them. It could thus be said that social responsibility is the implementation corollary of solidarity. Most religions enjoin on their followers that those who are "privileged" have an obligation to the disadvantaged. The term "privilege" does not imply wealth but is relative, and can be taken to connote a more fortunate situation in which one is placed than that of those who are disadvantaged.

EVOLUTION, PEACE AND NONVIOLENCE

The values and principles mentioned so far are not only basic values underpinning the concept of human rights, but also determining factors for the quality of interpersonal relations. Peace as a distinct vake, and not simply the absence of organised conflict, is one additional value.

Conflicts in human relations are unavoidable but ways to resolve them can be either peaceful or violent, constructive or destructive. The revolutionary, "rase all and build anew" approach has held 'sensation for people over the centuries, invariably at the cost of imposed and untold human suffering. It is an approach often chosen by social workers for the resolution of interpersonal and intergroup conflicts. Confrontation and resistance in the quest for freedom, justice and social justice are not eschewed; violence is.

History has shown time and again thrive violence and bloodshed bring about short-lived results and pave the way for more revolutions to dislodge newly enthroned power groups—the oppressed of yesterday.

While the world is not ready to abandon the use of arms, and just causes for revolution undoubtedly exist, it should be recognised that arbitration aid conciliation are effective tools to overcome seemingly irreconcilable differences provided they are practised consistently and with respect, understanding and knowledge.

Relations between Humankind and Nature

Respect for other species and a quest for harmony with nature are beginning to permeate human consciousness on the eve of the twenty-first century. Environmental degradation is too evident to be ignored. Excessive consumerism and extreme poverty endanger nature as well as vulnerable groups of people through greed, lack of information or need for survival. Comprehensive policies to halt and, where possible, repair damage to the environment need to be complemented by comprehensive environmental education programes, both formal and informal, as well as advocacy campaigns.

Human rights are universal and apply to all persons without discrimination. Respect for individual rights needs to be upheld at all times, irrespective of circumstances or political systems. The rights of any particular individual or group in any particular circumstances can be restricted only if they threaten to curtail similar or comparable rights of others.

It is important to consider the widespread notion of three human rights generations, of which the first, labelled "negative rights", represents civil and political rights as set forth in articles 2 to 21 of the Universal Declaration of Human Rights. These are rights devised to ensure freedom from any curtailment of individual liberty. The second generation encompasses the so-called "positive" rights found in articles 22 to 27 of the Declaration, which are aimed at ensuring social justice, freedom from want and participation in the social, economic and cultural aspects of life. The third generation comprises the "collective" rights embryonically indicated in article 28 of trie Declaration, which states that "Everyone is entitled to a social and international order in which the rights and freedoms set forth in this Declaration can be fully realised". In developing countries, the sheer proportion of need, and possibly of exploitation, leads to the collective vision of the right to social and economic development beyond the personal le vel to the national and regional levels, with a system of international solidarity for development as its ultimate aim.

In an increasingly interdependent world, recognition of the interdependence of the three human rights generations is gaining momentum. Although human rights are enshrined in separate international in.truments, they are perceived as forming a whole. A definition of human duties to be observed alongside human rights needs to be added to this perception.

WHAT IS SOCIAL WORK?

Social work originates variously from humanitarian and democratic ideals. Social work practice has since its beginning been focused on meeting human needs and on developing human potential and resources. "Social work is a profession whose purpose is to bring about social changes in society in general and in its individual forms of development." Professional social workers are dedicated to service for the welfare and selffulfilment of human beings;

Social workers are involved in planning, estimating, applying, evaluating and modifying preventive social policies and services to groups and communities. Social work education is aimed at promoting social development and worldwide quality education, training and knowledge for social work practice, social services, and social welfare politics.

Social work is always practised in five contexts which, while they may be analysed separately, are part of a whole. These contexts are geographical, political, socio-economic, cultural and spiritual.

(a) Geographical. All practice is located within some set of boundaries: agency, nation, State, region.

(b) Political. Every country has a political system. This sets the context for practice, whether the system is liberal or repressive, socialist, social democratic or capitalist.

(c) Socio-economic. An adequate livelihood, work, health and facilities, education and, if possible, access to social security and social services are basic human aspirations.

(d) Cultural. The practices, beliefs, aspirations and culture of individuals, families, groups, communities and nations have to be respected, though without prejudice to the evolution of certain practices and beliefs.

(e) Spiritual. No society in which social work is practised is value-free. It is central to social work/human practice that attention is paid to the spirit, the values, the philosophies, the ethics, and the hopes and ideals of those with whom social workers work and, at the same time, to social workers' own values.

Analysis of these five contexts reinforces the essential connectedness and coherence of social workers' efforts and the solidarity and energy of those who join in common cause in human rights work. Paying attention to geographical, political, socio-economic, cultural and spiritual contexts gives conscious direction to social work striving and practice, and makes manifest the human rights components in social work.

The profession's focus on human needs shapes its conviction that the fundamental nature of these needs requires that they be met not as a matter of choice but as an imperative of basic justice. Thus social work moves to a consideration of human rights as the other organising principle for its professional practice. The transition from needs orientation to rights affirmation has been made necessary because of tangible substantive needs that have to be met.

It follows that the search for and realisation of positive rights and entitlements is an inseparable twin to the meeting of needs. Working within different political systems, social workers uphold and defend the rights of their individual or collective clients while attempting to meet their needs. The profession's need to serve as a faithful employee has had to live alongside its obligation to serve the consumer of its practice. According to the profession's code of ethics and mission statements of schools of social 'work, service to people is the higher consideration.

Social work is concerned with the protection of individual and group differences. It is often forced to mediate between the people and the State and other authorities, to champion particular causes, and to provide protection when State action for the public good threatens the rights and freedoms of particular persons or groups.

As a bridging profession, social work has to be conscious of its values and possess a solid knowledge base, not least in the field of human rights, to guide it in many conflicting situations throughout the; practice. Viewing its work from a global human rights perspective helps the profession by providing a sense of unity and solidarity, without losing sight of the local perspectives, conditions and needs which constitute the framework within which social workers operate.

More than many professionals, social work educators and practitioners are conscious that the x concerns are closely linked to respect for human rights. They accept the premise that human rights and fundamental freedoms are indivisible, and that the full realisation of civil and political rights is impossible without enjoyment of economic, social and cultural rights. Their direct knowledge of the conditions of the vulnerable sectors of society makes social work educators and practitioners valuable in the formulation of social policies.

Human rights are inseparable from social work theory, values and ethics, and practice. Rights corresponding to human needs have to be upheld and fostered, and they embody the justification and motivation for social work action.

Human rights and social work have to be considered within the context of conditions faced by the majority of people on Earth at the close of the twentieth century. It is estimated that, in the past decade alone, more people lost their lives as a result of economic and social deprivation than perished in the Second World War.

Countless people have been killed or tortured or have disappeared in a world subjected to domination and oppression. Exploitative and oppressive systems and structures give rise to dictatorships and authoritarian regimes under which millions become victims of human rights violations as the price of their struggle for freedom and survival.

Each year 12.9 million children from developing countries die before the age of five and, in many of these countries, almost half the adult population is illiterate. Worldwide there are an estimated 17.5 million refugees and more than 25 million people displaced within their own countries because of civil strife, famine or other disaster. Close to 80 per cent of all refugees are women and children and, in some countries, women and children constitute 90 per cent of the refugee population.

Women are prominent in the statistics of poverty and deprivation. Two-thirds of the world's illiterate people are women. Maternal mortality rates are high in most developing countries.

While there are a few signs of progress following the end of the cold war, on the whole the crisis continues unabated, and in some parts of the world it has escalated. Almost one third of the total population in developing countries, or 1.3 billion people, live in absolute poverty, while nearly 1 billion are illiterate. Military spending is about 15 per cent of gross national product in the industrialised countries as well as in the developing countries. Each year, capital and interest repayments of $143 billion fall due. Even partial repayments made by the poorer nations jeopardise their social and economic development and cause great hardship to the poorest segments of their populations. According to World Bank estimates, the staggering debt burden of the developing counties amounting to $1.3 trillion, is likely to increase further.

Bilateral and multilateral aid programes serve to stave off some of the nefarious effects of the world recession on low-income countries. However, the World Bank predicts a "limited aid pie" in real terms throughout the 1990s. On the positive side, the Baik notes changed donor considerations, including environmental protection, efficient economic management, reduced military spending and the observance of human rights and the rule of law.

Facts and figures cited above are likely to remain accurate for a number of years. Attitudes, however, are changing. Ultimately, hope for improvement lies in human rights instruments and their implementation, and in evergrowing international consciousness and solidarity.

Basic Human Rights Instruments

United Nations bodies formulate international standards in the field of human rights by adopting or proclaiming recommendations called "declarations" or by preparing and opening for signature, ratification and accession multilateral treaties called "conventions".

A declaration is a formal and solemn instrument enunciating general principles and broad obligations. It is not a binding instrument and does not impose specific obligations on Member States.

Consequently, a declaration may by custom become recognised as laying down rules binding upon States.

In addition to the declaration, the United Nations soon developed international agreements (conventions) containing provisions to promote or protect specific human rights or fundamental freedoms. A convention enters into force only after having been ratified by a number of States as specified in the text.

In the field of human rights, United Nations bodies frequently adopt both declarations and conventions on a particular subject. In such a case, the declaration sets out general principles or general standards of human rights while the convention defines specific rights and limitations or restrictions on the use thereof, and sets out the obligations to be assumed by States which ratify or accede to it.

Basic Instruments Concerning Human Rights

Instruments Providing General Protection

(i) Charter of the United Nations (1945)

Born as the Second World War came to an end, the United Nations symbolised the determination of the world community to fashion new instruments to promote peace.

The international community accepted an obligation to establish guarantees for human rights which would afford protection to individuals, groups and communities whose rights were threatened by governmental action. Domestic jurisdictions were subordinated to the primacy of international jurisdiction in these key areas, and a framework developed to secure international protection.

(ii) Universal Declaration of Human Rights (1948)

The ringing phrases of the Universal Declaration represented the highest aspirations of humankind. It was expressed in terms that are non-political and set out the treatment that everyone in the world would be able to expect as a member of the human family. The instrument drew together for the first time ideas shared by many political, cultural and religious traditions.

The Universal Declaration sets out in its 30 articles the basic rules and freedoms for all peoples, covering civil, political, economic, social and cultural rights. Yet, in itself, the Declaration has no legal force. It is a set of moral rules.

(iii) International Covenants on Human Rights (1966)

The two Covenants derived from the Universal Declaration set out an internationally recognised standard against which human rights violations can be judged. The Covenants were adopted in 1966. The need for further work to secure the adherence of Member States to the principles set out in the Universal Declaration had long been recognised, but it took 18 years before the United Nations adopted the two Covenants and the implementation mechanisms attached to them.

The Covenants are of critical importance. They have three common elements: (a) the right to self determination, a right which has led to decolonisation and to many new States joining the United Nations; (b) the principle of equality between men and women, and non-discrimination on grounds of gender race or religion; (c) the principle of indivisibility.

(a) International Covenant on Civil and Political Rights (1966)

This instrument came into force in 1976. The rights set out therein include:

(a) The right to life, liberty and security;
(b) The right not to be subjected to torture or to cruel, inhuman or degrading treatment or punishment.
(c) The prohibition of slavery.
(d) The right not to be arbitrarily detained.
(e) The rights to freedom of expression, religion, assembly and association, including trade union membership;
(f) The right to freedom of movement an 1 residence.
(g) The right to vote through universal suffrage.
(h) The right to a fair trial and
(i) The rights of minorities to protection.

(b) International Covenant on Economic Social and Cultural Rights (1966)

This instrument came into force in 1976. The rights set out therein include:

(a) The right to work.

(b) The right to social security.

(c) The right to protection of the family.

(d) The right to an adequate standard of living.

(e) The right to education.

(/) The right to healthEnvironmental and

(g) The right to join trade unions.

What are the key elements for social workers in these three international instruments? The threat to civil and political freedoms is recognised in the work of the IFSW Human Rights Commission, which seeks to protect social workers threatened by political oppression.

Instruments Providing Particular Protection

(i) International Convention on the Elimination of All Forms of Racial Discrimination (1965)

The full enjoyment by everyone of the principle of equality and nondiscrimination is assured by the International Convention on the Elimination of All Forms of Racial Discrimination, which contains provisions for eliminating racial discrimination in all its forms and manifestations, for preventing and combating racist doctrines and practices and for building an international community free from all forms of racial segregation and discrimination.

The States parties to the Convention undertake to prohibit and to eliminate racial discrimination in all its forms and to guarantee the right of everyone, without distinction as to race, colour or national or ethnic origin, to equality before the law, notably in the enjoyment of a long list of human rights and fundamental freedoms.

(ii) Convention on the Elimination of All Forms of Discrimination against Women (1979)

From 1974 to 1979, the competent bodies of the United Nations led by the Commission on the Status of Women worked together for the elaboration of an international convention that would forbid all forms of discrimination against women. The Commission drafted a convention which was adopted on 18 December 1979 and entered into force in 1981.

In article 1, the Convention defines discrimination against women as meaning any distinction, exclusion or restriction made on the basis of sex which has the effect or purpose of impairing or nullifying the recognition, enjoyment or exercise by women, irrespective of their marital status, on a basis of equality of men and women, of human rights and fundamental freedoms in the political, economical, social, cultural, civil or any other field.

Under article 2, States that become parties to the Convention agree to pursue, by all appropriate means and without delay, a policy of eliminating discrimination against women, and to that end undertake:

(a) To embody the principle of equality of men and women in their national constitutions and to ensure, through law and other appropriate means, the practical realisation of this principle;

(b) To adopt appropriate legislative and other measures, including sanctions where appropriate, prohibiting all discrimination against women;

(c) To establish legal protection of the rights of women on an equal basis with men and to ensure, through competent national tribunals, tie effective protection of women against any act of discrimination;

(d) To take all appropriate measures to eliminate discrimination against women by any person, organisation or enterprise;

(e) To modify consequently or abolish law;, regulations, customs and practices which constitute discrimination against women.

(iii) Convention against Torture and other Cruel Inhuman or Degrading Treatment or Punishment (1984)

The Convention not only provides that the States parties will outlaw torture in their national legislation, but also notes explicitly that no order from a superior or exceptional circumstance may be invoked as a justification of torture or other cruel, inhuman or degrading treatment or punishment. The Convention a so introduces two new elements of particular importance to combat torture. The first is that, henceforth, a torturer may be prosecuted wherever he is found in this territory of any State party. The other new element is that the Convention contains a provision allowing for an international inquiry if there is reliable information indicating that torture is being systematically practised in the territory of a State party.

The States parties to the Convention also pledge to take effective legislative, administrative, judicial and other measures to prevent acts of torture in any territory under their jurisdiction. No exceptional circumstances whatever, whether a state of war, internal political instability or any other public emergency, may be invoked as a justification of torture.

(iv) Convention on the Rights of the Child (1989)

The Convention is the result of long negotiations between representatives of countries with different social and economic systems and various cultural, ethical and religious approaches; non-governmental organisations; and United Nations agencies. It has as its guiding spirit the best interests of the child aid calls on States which ratify it to create conditions in which children may take an active and creative part in the social and political life of their countries.

In the Convention, a child is defined as a person under the age of 18, unless national laws determine an earlier age of majority. Encompassing the whole range of human rights the Convention recognises that the enjoyment of a given right cannot be separated from the enjoyment of others. It demonstrates that the freedom a child needs to develop his or her intellectual, moral and spiritual capacities is dependent on a healthy and safe environment, access to care, and minimum standards of food, clothing and shelter, among other things. Non-discrimination is an important principle of the Convention.

The Convention enlarges the legal coverage of human rights by protecting children from all forms of exploitation in dealing with the question of children of minority and indigenous groups and the problems of drug abuse and neglect. The Convention acknowledges the primary role of the family and parents in the care and protection of children, and the obligation of the State to help them carry out these duties. The implementation of the Convention is entrusted to the Committee on the Rights of the Child.

(v) International Convention on the Protection of the Rights of All Migrant Workers and Members of Their Families (1990)

Migrant workers and their families who are usually not citizens of the country in which they live and work have for some years been of particular concern to the United Nations and specialised agencies. In 1979, the General Assembly decided to establish a working group open to all Member States to elaborate an international convention on the protection of the rights of all migrant workers and their families. The Convention is applicable to all migrant workers and members of their families without distinction of any kind such as sex, race, colour, language, religion or conviction, political or other opinion, national, ethnic or social origin, age, economic position, property, marital status, birth or other status. The monitoring of the application of the Convention, when it enters into force, will be entrusted to the Committee on the Protection of the Rights of All Migrant Workers and Members of Their Families.

Rules Regarding Detention and Treatment of Offenders

(i) Standard Minimum Rules for the Treatment of Prisoners

In 1955, the First United Nations Congress on the Prevention of Crime and the Treatment of Offenders adopted a set of standard minimum rules for the treatment of prisoners and the management of penal institutions. In 1971, the General Assembly recommended that the rules be effectively implemented in the administration of penal and correctional institutions and that favourable consideration be given to their corporation into national legislation.

(ii) Principles of Medical Ethics (1982)

In 1976, the General Assembly invited the World Health Organisation to draft a code of medical ethics relevant to the protection of persons subjected to any form of detention or imprisonment. With the assistance of WHO, the Council for International Organisations of Medical Sciences and the World Medical Assembly, the General Assembly formulated and adopted in 1982 a set of Principles of Medical Ethics against torture and other cruel, inhuman or degrading treatment or punishment relevant to the roe of health personnel, particularly physicians, in the protection of prisoners and detainees.

(iii) United Nations Standard Minimum Rules for the Administration of Juvenile Justice (1985)

In 1985, the Seventh United Nations Congress on the Prevention of Crime and the Treatment of Offenders prepared and recommended to the General Assembly for adoption the United Nations Standard Minimum Rules for the Administration of Juvenile Justice, or the "Beijing Rules". The rules relate to such matters as the minimum age of criminal responsibility, the, objectives of juvenile justice, the features of effective, fair and humane juvenile justice administration and the human rights principles to be applied. In general, they recommend the e least possible use of institutionalisation. They also key down essential protection covering juvenile offenders placed in institutions. The General Assembly adopted the rules in 1985 and invited States to apply them wherever necessary and bring them to the attention of relevant authorities and the public in general.

Specialised Agencies

(i) International Labour Organisation

The International Labour Organisation was established in 1919 as an autonomous institution to promote programes to achieve full employment and raise standards of living. The organisation is concerned with both economic and social rights, such as the right to work, the right to the enjoyment of just and favourable conditions of work, the right to form trade unions and join the trade union of one's choice, the right to social security and the right to an adequate standards of living. It endeavours to implement the principles of its Constitution by laying down standards, supervising their application and assisting Governments to achieve ELO objectives.

Among the more than 170 conventions adopted by LLO, the following is a representative list of instruments with a strong human rights component:

— Forced labour, adopted in 1930
— Equal remuneration (1951)
— Abolition of forced labour (1957)
— Discrimination (1958)
— Employment policy (1964)
— Minimum age for employment and work (1973)
— Rural workers' organisations (1975)
— Migrant workers (1975)
— Workers with family responsibilities (1981)
— Indigenous and tribal peoples (1989).

(ii) United Nations Educational, Scientific and Cultural Organisation

The United Nations Educational, Scientific and Cultural Organisation has for many years taken the lead in giving concrete meaning to the right to participate in cultural life enshrined in article 27 of the Universal Declaration of Human Rights. Thus, in 1966, the General Conference of UNESCO adopted and proclaimed the Declaration of the Principles of International Cultural Cooperation. Some of these principles are set out below:

(a) Each culture has a dignity and value which must be respected and preserved;

(b) Every people has the right and the duty to develop its culture;

(c) Nations shall endeavour to develop the various branches of culture side by side, and as far as possible simultaneously.

(d) International cultural cooperation shall cover all aspects of intellectual and creative activities relating to education, science and culture;

(e) Cultural cooperation is a right and a duty for all peoples and all nations, which should share with one another their knowledge and skills;

(f) International cooperation, while promoting the enrichment of all cultures through its beneficent action, shall respect the distinctive character of each.

In education, its main activity, UNESCO combines literacy programes with a drive to make primary education universal, thereby attacking the root causes of illiteracy. It also trains teachers, educational planners and administrators to encourage local building and equipping of schools. This action is based on the Recommendation concerning Education for International Understanding, Cooperation and Peace and Education relating to Human Rights and Fundamental Freedoms adopted by the General Conference in 1974.

(iii) World Health Organisation

The World Health Organisation is a specialised agency which cooperates closely with the other: competent bodies in the United Nations system in dealing with matters relating to the right to health as proclaimed in article 25, paragraph 1, of the Universal Declaration of Human Rights.

The Constitution of WHO, adopted in 1946, states that "the enjoyment of the highest available standard of health is one of the fundamental rights of every human being without distinction as to race, religion, political belief, economic or social situation". It defines health as "a state of complete physical, mental and social well-being and not merely the absence of disease or infirmity".

WHO carries out important campaigns to combat communicable diseases. In developing countries, it also carries out an extensive technical assistance programe covering every aspect of public health, as well as teaching and training health personnel. Since 1989, WHO has developed a programe on ADDS and human rights in cooperation with the United Nations Centre for Human Rights.

United Nations Bodies

(i) Office of the United Nations High Commissioner for Refugees

The United Nations has been concerned since its inception with the situation of refugees, displaced persons, stateless persons and returnees and has adopted a number of measures to protect their human rights and find appropriate and lasting solutions to their problems. Consequently, at its fourth session, in 1949, the; General Assembly established the Office of the United Nations High Commissioner for Refugees, which replaced the International Refugee Organisation set up after the Second World War.

Such protection activity is developed in accordance with the 1951 Convention relating to the Status of Refugees and its 1967 Protocol. The Convention sets out in article 1 a definition of the term "refugee". Articles 2 to 11 contain general provisions and provide for non-discrimination as to race, religion or country of origin. Articles 12 to 16 pertain to the juridical status of the refugee. Articles 17 to 19 concern the rights of refugees to engage in gainful employment. Articles 20 to 24 concern the welfare of the refugee in regard to such matters as rationing, housing, public education, public relief, labour legislation and social security.

Article 25 deals with the provision of administrative assistance to refugees and of documents to enable them to travel outside their country of lawful residence. Articles 31 to 33 contain important provisions relating to the question of asylum. According to these articles, a refugee requesting asylum in the territory of a contracting State may not be subjected to penalties on account of his illegal entry or presence, provided he presents himself without delay to the competent authorities. In any event, he may not be expelled or returned in any manner whatsoever to the frontiers of territories where his life or freedom would be threatened on account of race, religion, nationality, membership of a particular social group or political opinion.

Article 34 of the Convention requires contracting States as far as possible to facilitate the assimilation and naturalisation of refugees. Lastly, article 35 requires contracting States to cooperate with UNHCR in the exercise of its functions and, in particular, to facilitate its duty of supervising the application of the provisions of the Convention.

In 1967, the General Assembly also adopted the Declaration on Territorial Asylum, which lays down a series of fundamental principles in regard to territorial asylum and gives expression to the basic humanitarian principle of "non-refoulement". According to that principle, no person shall be rejected at the frontier, expelled or returned to a country where he may be subjected to persecution.

(ii) United Nations Children's Fund

The United Nations Children's Fund was created by the General Assembly at its first session in 1946 to meet the emergency needs of children for food, drugs and clothing in postwar Europe and China. In 1950, the Assembly changed the main emphasis of the Fund's mandate to programes of long-range benefits to children of developing countries. Three ye..rs later, the Assembly decided that UNICEF should continue this work indefinitely.

Combining humanitarian and development objectives, UNICEF cooperates with developing countries in their efforts to protect children and enable them to develop their full potential. In order to respond to emergency needs of children in Central and Eastern Europe and in the former Soviet Union, UNICEF is also providing assistance to some countries in that region.

UNICEF collaborates closely with the Committee on the Rights of the Child, which pronotes children's rights, monitors the implementation of the Convention and assists States which ratify or accede to the Convention to comply with their obligations.

(iii) United Nations Environment Programe

The United Nations Conference on the Human Environment held at Stockholm in 1972 proclaimed the right of human beings to a healthy environment and their responsibility to protect and improve that environment for future generations.

Later in 1972, the General Assembly created the United Nations Environment Programe to monitor the environment and encourage sound environmental practices. UNEP's main task is to act as a catalyst for the environmental activities of all United Nations agencies.

In 1989, UNEP negotiated the Basal Convention on the Control of Transboundary Movements of Hasardous Wastes and their Disposal. The main international instruments in the field of the environment were promulgated by the United Nations Conference on Environment and Development in June 1992, namely the United Nations Framework Convention on Climate Change and the Convention on Biological Diversity, as well as Agenda 21 and the Rio Declaration. The Commission on Sustainable Development set up to monitor the effective implementation of Agenda 21 started its work in June 1993.

United Nations Bodies Concerned with Human Rights

(i) General Assembly and Subsidiary Bodies

Under Article 13 of the Charter of the United Nations, one of the functions of the General Assembly is to initiate studies and make recommendations for "promoting international cooperation in the economic, social, cultural, educational and health fields, and assisting in the realisation of human rights and fundamental freedoms for all without distinction as to race, sex, language or religion".

(ii) Economic and Social Council and Subsidiary Bodies

Under Article 62 of the Charter of the United Nations, the Economic and Social Council may "make recommendations for the purpose of promoting respect for, and observance of, human rights and fundamental freedoms for all". Under Article 68, the Council "shall set up commissions in economic and social fields and for the promotion of human rights". To assist it in dealing with items relating to human rights, the Council has established the Commission on Human Rights.

(a) Commission on Human Rights

Established by the Economic and Social Council in 1946, the Commission on Human Rights, composed of representatives of 56 member States elected for three-year terms, meets each year for a period of six weeks. The Commission makes studies, prepares recommendations and drafts international instruments relating to human rights.

During their annual sessions, the Commission on Human Rights, the Economic and Social Council and the General Assembly discuss situations and practices involving serious and systematic violations of human rights. If a particular "country" situation or a particular practice is deemed sufficiently serious, they may decide to order an investigation by either a group of independent and objective experts (working group) or an individual (special rapporteur). In cases requiring urgent attention, the special rapporteur or working group may even be able to communicate immediately with the Government concerned in an effort to protect the individual, group or community under threat.

The first special procedure—established in 1967—was the Ad Hoc Working Group on Human Rights in Southern Africa. Several other special procedures established by the Commission were discontinued when human rights in the countries concerned improved.

Since 1980, the Commission has established special procedures to study and take action in relation to practices involving grave human rights violations all over the world. These are called "thematic mediates". At present, there are two thematic working groups: one on enforced or involuntary disappearances and the other on arbitrary detention. There are also eight thematic special rapporteurs: on extrajudicial, summary or arbitrary executions; on torture and other cruel, inhuman or degrading treatment or punishment; on sale of children, child prostitution and child pornography; on internally displaced persons; on religious intolerance; on racism, racial discrimination and xenophobia; on freedom of opinion and expression; and on the use of mercenaries as a means of impeding the right of peoples to self-determination.

(b) *Sub-Commission on Prevention of Discrimination and Protection of Minorities*

In order to carry out its work more efficiently, the Commission on Human Rights established, in 1947, the Sub-Commission on Prevention of Discrimination and Protection of Minorities, to undertake studies, particularly in the light of the Universal Declaration of Human Rights, and to make recommendations to the Commission concerning the prevention of discrimination of any kind relating to human rights and fundamental freedoms and the protection of racial, religious and linguistic minorities. Governmental organisations. United Nations specialised agencies and national liberation movements concerned with issues on its agenda.

(c) Commission on the Status of Women

The Commission on the Status of Women was established by the Economic and Social Council in 1946. Its functions are to prepare recommendations and reports to the Council on promoting women's rights in the political, economic, civil, social and educational fields, and to make recommendations and proposals for action on urgent problems in the field of women's right! The Commission has been given the task of monitoring, reviewing and appraising the implementation of the Nairobi Forward-looking Strategies for the Advancement of Women adopted by the 1985 World Conference on women. No action is taken on individual complaints. Instead, the procedure aims to discern emerging trends and patterns of discrimination against women in order to develop policy recommendations for solving widespread problems.

(iii) Centre for Human Rights

Secretariat services for United Nations bodies dealing with human rights are provided by the Centre for Human Rights, which is located at the United Nations Office at Geneva with a small liaison office at United Nations Headquarters in New York. The main functions of the Centre for Human Rights are to assist the General Assembly, the Economic and Social Council, the Commission on Human Rights and other organs of the United Nations in the promotion and protection of human rights and fundamental freedoms as envisaged in the Charter of the United Nations, the Universal Declaration of Human Rights and international conventions in the field of human rights.

The Centre serves as the focal point of the United Nations in the field of human rights. It carries out research and studies on human rights at the request of other organs, follows up and prepares reports on the implementation of human rights, and administers the programe of advisory services and technical assistance in the field of human rights.

Implementation Mechanisms

(i) Human Rights Committee

Established in 1977, the Human Rights Committee monitors the implementation of the International Covenant on Civil and Political Rights. It is composed of 18 members, elected by States parties to the Covenant from among their nationals, who serve in their personal capacity. The Committee holds three sessions a year to consider reports from States parties to the Covenant on measures adopted and progress made towards achieving observance of the rights recognised in the Covenant.

(ii) Committee on Economic, Social and Cultural Rights

The Committee on Economic, Social and Cultural Rights monitors the implementation of the International Covenant on Economic, Social and Cultural Rights. It held its first session in 1987 and is composed of 18 experts with recognised competence in the field of human rights who serve in their personal capacity.

(iii) Committee on the Elimination of Racial Discrimination

The Committee on the Elimination of Racial Discrimination, which monitors the implementation of the International Convention on the Elimination of All Forms of Racial Discrimination, is composed of 18 members elected by States parties to the Convention for a four-year term. The Committee is also authorised to establish permanent working groups and/or ad hoc conciliation commissions to consider communications from individual:; and inter-State disputes relating to obligations contained in the Convention.

(iv) Committee on the Elimination of Discrimination against Women

The Committee on the Elimination of Discrimination against Women was established to oversee the implementation of the Convention on the Elimination of All Forms of Discrimination against Women. The Committee meets regularly to examine reports and any other information submitted by States parties. This examination farms the basis of suggestions and recommendations made by the Committee. The Committee may also make general recommendations on steps which might be taken by States to fulfil their obligations under the Convention.

(v) Committee against Torture

The Committee against Torture is imposed of 10 experts elected for a four-year term to consider reports submitted by States parties to the Convention against Torture and Other Cruel, Inhuman or Degrading Treatment or Punishment on measures taken to honour their undertakings under the Convention. In addition to considering these reports, investigating them and forwarding them to the States parties and to the General Assembly with comments, the Committee is authorised to make confidential inquiries. These may include on-the-spot inquiries, in agreement with the State party concerned, when the Committee receives reliable information indicating that torture is being systematically practised in the territory of that State party.

The United Nations Voluntary Fund for Victims of Torture was set up in 1981 to receive voluntary contributions for distribution through establish ;d channels of assistance as humanitarian, legal and financial aid to persons who have been tortured and to members of their families. It is administered by the Secretary-General of the United Nations with the assistance of a board of trustees composed of a chairperson and four members with wide experience in the field of human rights.

(vi) Committee on the Rights of the Child

The Committee on the Rights of the Child first met in 1991. It is composed of 10 experts and is entrusted with the task of generating a permanent dialogue involving all parties concerned with the promotion of children's rights. The Committee will identify dangers to the well-being of the world's children; look for practical answers to specific problems; mobilise the human and financial resources needed to solve them; and raise the level of public awareness and concern for the protection and promotion of the rights of the child. States parties to the Convention accept the duty to submit regular reports directly to the Committee on the steps they have taken to put the Convention into effect and on progress in securing the enjoyment of children's rights. These reports are to be made public and given wide national distribution.

Regional Instruments in the Held of Human Rights

(i) Africa

(a) Charter of the Organisation of African Unity (1963)

The OAU Charter was the first instrument of a regional organisation to refer to the Universal Declaration of Human Rights. Its preamble reaffirms the attachment of the African States to the principles of the Charter of the United Nations and the Universal Declaration of Human

Rights as a solid foundation for peaceful and positive cooperation among States. Article II provides for the promotion of international cooperation with regard to the United Nations Charter and the Universal Declaration.

(b) African Charter on Human and Peoples' Rights (1981)

The African Charter on Human and Peoples' Rights comprises a preamble and three substantive parts containing 68 articles. Part I, dealing with rights and duties, is subdivided into two chapters on human and peoples' rights and duties. Part II, containing measures of safeguard, is subdivided into four chapters dealing with the creation of the African Commission on Human and Peoples' Rights the mandate of the Commission, its procedure and applicable principles.

(c) African Commission on Human and People!' Rights

The main functions of the Commission are promotional and standard-setting. The Commission also receives and considers inter-State and "other communications". The latter term includes communications from individuals or groups of individuals and from organisations or institutions dealing with human rights issues.

(ii) The Americas

(a) Charter of the Organisation of American States—American Declaration of the Rights and. Duties of Man (1948)

The OAS Charter, which entered into force in 1951, makes very few references to human rights. One provision of importance is article 3, now article 5 proclaiming the fundamental rights of the individual without distinction as to race, nationality, creed or sex among the principles to which signatories are committed. Another important reference to human rights appears in article 13, now article 16.

(b) American Convention on Human Rights '1969)

The American Convention on Human Rights guarantees a dozen broad categories of civil and. political rights, such as the right to judicial personality and the right to life, to humane treatment, to a fair trial, to property, and to freedom of association, among others. An additional protocol to the Convention, relating to economic, social and cultural rights and known as the San Salvador Protocol, was adopted in 1988.

(c) Supervisory organs (i) Inter-American Commission on Human Rights

The functions of the Commission are snelled out in article 41 of the American Convention or Human Rights. It codifies the Commission's pre-existing functions as an OAS organ and mandates it "to take action on petitions and other communications pursuant to its authority" under articles 44 to 51 of the Convention. The admissibility of a petition is conditional, inter alia, on the exhaustion of domestic remedies, in accordance with the generally recognised principles of international law. There is a requirement that the petition be submitted to the Commission within a period of six months from the date on which the victim of the alleged violation was notified of the final domestic judgement in the case. When a complaint is admissible, the Commission examines the allegations, seeks information from the Government concerned and investigates the facts.

(d) Inter-American Court of Human Rights

The Court has contentious jurisdiction, which is jurisdiction to adjudicate cases involving charges that a State party has violated the American Convention on Human Rights. The Court is empowered to award money dam ages and render declaratory judgements specifying not only what rights have been violated, but also how States should remedy the violation.

(iii) Europe

(a) European. Convention on Human Rights (1950)

As originally adopted, the European Convention on Human Rights guaranteed a wide range of rights, such as the right to life, the right not to be subjected to torture, and freedom from slavery, among others. This range has been expanded by additional protocols to add the right to property and the right to education. Protocols 4 and 5 expand the list further by prohibiting deprivation of liberty for failure to comply with contractual obligations and guaranteeing the right to liberty of movement. Protocol 6 requires abolition of the death penalty, and Protocol 7 requires that aliens must be accorded various due procedural safeguards in determining whether they may be expelled from a country where they are residing.

(b) European Social Charter (1961)

Like the European Convention, the European Social Charter was prepared under the auspices of the Council of Europe. More than half the member States of the Council of Europe are parties to the Charater. The Charter establishes a reporting system designed to monitor whether States are complying with their obligations.

(c) Conference on Security and Cooperation in Europe

The Helsinki Final Act, signed in 1975, grew out of the Conference on Security and Cooperation in Europe (CSCE), which grouped all sovereign States of Eastern and Western Europe, together with the United States of America and Canada. It is not binding on Governments, although it has had considerable political impact. Among subsequent important CSCE documents are the concluding documents of the Vienna (1989) and Copenhagen (1990) conferences, as well as the Charter of Paris for a New Europe (1990).

(d) European Court of Human Rights

Initially, the European Convention conferred only contentious jurisdiction on the Europe in Court of Human Rights. The Court obtained advisory jurisdiction in 1970, with the entry into force of Protocol 2 to the Convention. However, the individual claimant has gradually acquired a more important status before the Court. The Court can be said to have become the constitutional court for civil liberties in Western Europe. Its case-law is vast in terms of the range of subjects the Court has addressed, and its impact is increasing.

Other Human Rights Instruments

(i) Declaration on the Right to Development (1986)

In 1986, the General Assembly adopted the Declaration on the Right to Development, which proclaims that development is an inalienable human right, entitling all persons to participate in, contribute to and enjoy economic, social, cultural and political development in which all human rights and fundamental freedoms can be fully realised.

(ii) Declaration on the Elimination of All Forms of Religious Intolerance (1981)

The Declaration on the Elimination of All Forms of Intolerance and of Discrimination Based on Religion or Belief was adopted by the General Assembly in 1981. It states that everyone shall have :he right to freedom of thought, conscience and religion and that no one shall be subject to discrimination on the grounds of religion or other belief.

(iii) Declaration on the Protection of Women and Children in Emergency and Armed Conflict (1974)

In 1974, the General Assembly proclaimed the Declaration on the Protection of Women and Children in Emergency and Armed Conflict. The Declaration states that attacks and bombings on civilians, "especially on women and children, who are the most vulnerable members of the population", shall be prohibited and condemned, and that States involved in armed conflicts shall make all efforts "to spare women and children from the ravages of war".

(iv) Declaration on the Rights of Mentally Retarded Persons (1971)

In 1971, the General Assembly proclaimed the Declaration on the Rights of Mentally Retarded Persons and called for national and international action to ensure that the Declaration would be used as a common basis and frame of reference for the protection of the rights set forth therein.

Issues in Teaching and Learning about Human Rights

Teaching and learning about human rights in a social work context is not fundamentally different from other subject areas. It requires application and analysis, as well as a personal commitment to communication and understanding.

Recognition of Human Rights Issues

Many aspects of social work, and the field of social work itself, have an implicit human rights dimension. The first requirement, for teachers and students, is to train themselves to recognise and explore these dimensions—both in theory and in practice.It is helpful always to consider the three levels of analysis prior to goal-setting in response to issues. Thought also needs to be given to using the preventive, developmental and social action approaches of social work intervention.

One traditional approach in social work is to begin with the individual person, perhaps in a family context. In a parallel way, many basic human rights issues also have their starting-point in the fundamental rights of individuals. However, this level of analysis needs to be supplemented by analysis at further levels.

Another approach to social problems, already practised in schools of social work, is to identify social problems or issues initially at the meso or macro level and explore the personal and organisational consequences as they impact on the work of social workers. For social work educators, practitioners and students, however, it is the range rather than the starting-point of analysis which is important, as is the incorporation of an ethical and human rights dimension.

Responding to Human Rights Issues

Following analysis, social workers need to respond. This section identifies a framework in general terms, although particular contexts will, of course, require different specifications.

(i) Recognition

Social workers need to recognise that *the/* are responding to a situation which includes a dimension of human rights. In other words, they need to conceptualise the situation by asking themselves questions such as: What human rights are at issue in this situation? What are the possible goals/means for changing this situation?

(ii) Prioritising

There may be several human rights issues, and possibly violations, involved in a given situation. Social workers may therefore have to examine relative priorities for intervention in conjunction with the;

persons concerned. This will lead to a process of goals setting in a specific context and in such a way that the achievement of goals can be evaluated. Goals will thus form part of a coherent strategy for responding to the situation from a human rights perspective.

Reference Groups for the Social Worker

Underpinning the execution of intervention strategies there needs to be support elements for the social worker. Support may be required from individuals, organisations, groups and movements involved in similar human rights issues. They might be solidarity groups, self-help groups, trade unions, professions, law-enforcement officials, specific non-governmental organisations, political parties, the churches, or others.

Evaluation

Intervention by social workers should be evaluated, at least in conjunction with the client and the social worker's supervisor. A specific evaluation of the action taken in response to human rights issues raised by the given situation should be built into this process.

Follow-up Action

After the (evaluated) outcome of the particular case, future action may need to be considered by the social worker and his or her agency in the light of the success or failure of previous strategies. Again, such action should be conceptualised at different levels and in different contexts. A practical means of promoting understanding of human rights could, *inter alia,* involve the agency's offer to train supervisors in short, medium or long-range planning and to facilitate data collection for future research.

Recognition of the Consequences of Human Rights Activity

For social workers, as for individuals, clients and groups, active engagement in promoting awareness, understanding and implementation of human rights can be harmful, dangerous, or even fatal, even if successful in achieving goals or improving respect for human rights. Students should be encourage i to be realistically aware of such consequences, which in some cases can cast a threatening shadow over many aspects of their work.

Students should also be encouraged to participate in national or specific committees of profession associations, or national or international non-governmental organisations in the field of human rights. Such participation will incidentally recognise the status md value of such work within this area, and counteract pressures to have it marginalised.

Maintaining the Profile of Human Rights Activity in Social Work

It is important that human rights activity in social work and social work education is not marginalised. This requires:

(a) Adoption of the principle of respect for human rights, and implementation in the practice of teaching human rights. This includes staff orientation and development.

(b) Maintenance of adequate teaching materials, including international human rights instruments, case-studies, innovatory research papers and other materials in schools of social work.

(c) Adequate funding for the human rights area of work.

(d) Review of existing course content, and revision/additions to take account of human rights issues.

(e) A programe for teaching staff and students, including presentations by human rights activists.

(J) Encouragement of outreach links/twinning of schools of social work with human rights organisations locally, nationally and internationally. Such links can involve reciprocal visits, placements, exchange of news, etc.

(g) Creation of awards and other forms of recognition for work in human rights and social work, including work undertaken by students, and recognition of victims of human rights violations.

(h) Integration of human rights concerns in action programes of schools of social work and professional social work organisations.

Field Work

Field work is an integral part of social work education which affords students the opportunity of witnessing the practical application of the theory learned from literature and in the classroom. It is therefore important that field instructors help students identify human rights aspects in everyday practice during their mandatory placements. Field assignments may vary according to the level of studies and are to be found in informal community settings as well as in agencies and institutions.

Conscious emphasis on the protection of the human rights of all persons with whom contacts are established during an assignment will provide depth to the learning process. It might therefore be worthwhile for schools to consider asking students to write reports on their field work from a human rights perspective.

The first, or in some cases renewed, involvement with social work practice is crucial. Much will depend on the knowledge and attitudes of both instructors and students. The limits and possibilities provided by social, economic and political systems; possible constraints of organisational structures; cultural traditions.

Research

Serious academic research in the field of social work and human rights is a key element for ensures knowledge of and respect for human rights in social work practice. This goes well beyond the evaluation of action undertaken by practitioners or students addressed earlier.

There is much research material in the field of human rights: causes of human rights violations; prevention of human rights abuses through awareness-raising, advocacy and social action, among other things; human rights education; legal measures to counter human rights abuses; sustained pressure at the political level; early-warning systems; and recognition and compensation for human rights victims are but some of the subjects which social work academics, practitioners and students could address.

Besides its scientific value, serious research could also set standards, be quoted or even be used is a yard-stick in cases of conflict and dispute involving a human rights issue.

References

Riessman, C. K. (2001) 'Personal Troubles as Social Issues: A Narrative of Infertility in Context', in I. Shaw and N. Gould (eds) *Qualitative Research in Social Work: Method and Context*, pp. 73–82. Newbury Park, CA: Sage.

Shaw, I. and Gould,N. (eds) (2001) *Qualitative Research in Social Work: Method and Context*. Newbury Park, CA: Sage.

Urek, M. (2005) 'Making a Case in Social Work: The Construction of an Unsuitable Mother', *Qualitative Social Work* 4(4): 451–67.

White, S. and Featherstone,B. (2005) 'Communicating Misunderstandings: Multi-agency Work as Social Practice', *Child and Family Social Work* 10: 207–16.

8

Social Care Services

Our society is based on the belief that everyone has a contribution to make and has the right to control their own lives. This value drives our society and will also drive the way in which we provide social care. Services should be person-centred, seamless and proactive. They should support independence, not dependence and allow everyone to enjoy a good quality of life, including the ability to contribute fully to our communities. They should treat people with respect and dignity and support them in overcoming barriers to inclusion. They should be tailored to the religious, cultural and ethnic needs of individuals.

While person-centred planning is extensively supported by Government, policy makers, commissioners and practitioners, and not least service users and their families, obstacles to its widespread implementation remain. This scoping review investigates what existing literature identifies as prevailing barriers and bridges to the implementation of person-centred planning in adult social care. It also examines person-centred planning from the perspectives of service users and their families, and from the perspective of frontline staff.

Person-centred Planning

Person-centred planning is based on learning through shared action, about finding creative solutions rather than fitting people into boxes and about problem solving and working together over time to create change in the person's life, in the community and in organisations.

Person-centred planning is an umbrella term referring to a variety of specific approaches to helping people who use social care services to plan their own futures It is a way in which support for people who use social care services can be organised as well as a way of enabling people to take a lead in planning all aspects of how the service they receive are delivered.

Person-centred planning is the result of nearly 30 years' dialogue and investigation. Having been developed in the US and Canada it has grown in importance in the UK. Its origins can be traced to changes that took place in the early 1970s as part of a move to 'normalisation' or ordinary living when long-stay institutions for disabled people began to close down.

Several terms are found in the literature that refer to what is described here as person-centred planning. The phrase person-centred planning is most commonly found in physical disability and learning difficulty literature, while, in the field of dementia care and services for older people, person-centred care is the term that tends to prevail. In the mental health literature the terminology relies on notions of empowerment and user inclusion, and tends to emphasise the philosophical foundations of support rather than routes for putting ideas into practice.

Discussions of person-centred planning appear in the literature to describe both a philosophical understanding of the concept and a range of practical approaches to offering support. There are several differing approaches to implementing person-centred planning but each shares characteristics that explicitly emphasise the personal empowerment of service users, in which the principal direction for support generates from those for whom planning is being carried out.Person-centred planning is grounded in a rights based approach incorporating principles of independence, choice and inclusion.

From a philosophical perspective person-centred planning involves a substantial shift in thinking from that which has long governed approaches to care. In the past the needs of disabled people were determined without reference to individuals, the assumption being that the needs of any particular user group were universally rather than individually defined. This mode of thinking meant that organisations took decisions for people about how they should live and the nature of the care they received.

Person-centred planning is a strong planning process that puts the person at the centre and deliberately shifts power towards them and can help reclaim some of the freedom which most of us take for granted.

This philosophy that underpins practice can be thought of as guiding principles of person-centred planning, and includes increased community access and inclusion, the development of relationships, greater opportunities for choice, the advancement of valued and respected roles, and the development of improved personal skills. Person-centred planning is about equality. It challenges the unequal power structures that have long reigned in the relationships between service providers and service users.

As a philosophy that espouses notions of choice, independence and inclusion, ideas embedded in the concept of person-centred planning inevitably influence the way that services should be designed. Rather than service users fitting into an existing universal service, a 'one size fits all' design, services should be designed to fit around the needs of individuals. The philosophy is therefore inseparable and continually influential on the practical implementation of person-centred planning. However, while changes in thinking are necessary within services for person-centred planning to become a reality, they are also necessary within wider society so that real progress can be made towards equality and justice for people who use social care services.

Implementation of person-centred planning relies heavily on a shift in thinking among managers and frontline staff about the way in which support is delivered. Processes to guide practice are needed and four tools have been developed for the implementation of person-centred planning. These include:

1 The McGill Action Planning System (MAPS)

2 ELP (Essential Lifestyle Planning)

3 Personal Futures Planning

4 PATHS (Planning Alternative Tomorrows and Hope).

It is not a single technique but a 'family' of approaches that, collectively, seek to give disabled people control over their own lives and ensure that they are respected and valued. Each has a particular approach that is appropriate for different individuals in different situations. Alternatively, a combination of approaches may be used or an individualised method that has drawn inspiration from the methods described briefly below. Stalker and Campbell provide a good overview of the key characteristics of each type of approach. The McGill Action Planning System (MAPS) brings together a group of people who help to identify the focus on service users' talents and needs, and to negotiate changes to their routines based on their desires and aspirations. This process is useful for gathering information and is often used at an early stage of planning.

Attention to the processes needed for the implementation of person-centred planning is important. It should take into account the particular needs of individuals, the aim of the plan, the particular communication style of the service user, others likely to be involved and individual personal preferences.

It should be noted that, although 'planning' features in the terminology, the plan is simply a first step: 'the plan is not the outcome'. Moreover, the plan itself should not be regarded as fixed and immutable over time, and adhered to in changing situations, but simply a guide in the moment, which needs continual review and updating in respect of the changing needs, decisions and desires of the service user.

Although each planning method has different features, common characteristics pertain. They all adopt a perspective that sees the whole person rather than seeing them merely from a medical or clinical point of view. Each strategy is orientated towards the future. Duffy and Sanderson identify five 'gears' of care management that can make use of person-centred planning and outline how the planning process 'matures' through:

1. Reaching an initial understanding
2. Agreeing goals
3. Making use of available resources
4. Implementing change
5. Reviewing, learning and amending.

Another important aspect of person-centred planning is the involvement of nonprofessionals in the processes of planning and implementation. People who use social care services are often isolated and to some degree excluded from the wider community. Person-centred planning emphasises finding ways to support communities to include everybody. This is reflected in policy, for instance in the Disability Discrimination Act (1995).

Sanderson considers family and friends to be partners in any planning process; however, she states that this is ultimately the decision of the service user. Circles of support are one way of involving non-professionals in the development and implementation of a person-centred plan. Sanderson contends that 'person-centred planning cannot be truly effective without a circle of support'. Other case study reports of person-centred planning set out less formal arrangements, particularly at the early stages.

R lived in a residential home with four others and had regular contact with his family. His first PCP [person-centred planning] meeting was designed as a type of party. His favourite food and lots of drink were prepared and a room was chosen so he could move around – run, jump, as he wished. His mother was initially asked if she would like to be the facilitator and told that she could be offered support through training if she wished but she felt a bit nervous about the process and the responsibility of this role, and thought it might happen at a later stage. The first meetings were initially facilitated by the care manager and then jointly with the key worker from the home.

Interpreting the Concept

Person-centred planning is central to many current policy initiatives relating to social and health care. This reflects a wider social trend towards a focus on individuality and an emphasis on the importance of promoting independence and autonomy. However, the notion of autonomy, individuality and independence may be at odds with ideas of societal responsibility, interdependence and community values. Nolan and his colleagues argue that, for tangible improvements in quality of life to be evident, then values other than independence and autonomy should predominate.

The language of person-centred planning implies that it resides in a 'community', which is not always found in the contemporary social environment. This points to a fundamental inconsistency within the notion of person-centred planning; while independence and autonomy are widely endorsed for users of social care services, for them to be realised there needs to be complementary community action that embraces interdependence and inclusion. Therefore, if person-centred planning relies on this imagined community, are we not simply continuing to endorse 'special needs' under the guise of 'ordinary lives'?

SERVICE DEVELOPMENTS

Social care services and support systems exist because of the needs of people who use them. However, the needs of service users have not always been central to the planning of services. Person-centred planning is now at the heart of the Government's strategy for people who use health and social care services

Traditionally, planning has sought to fit people into existing services. Such services have often taken a philosophical stance that regards service users as passive recipients of care, who do not need to know what lies behind its organisation and do not need to be involved or take an active part in the development of services.

Stainton examines past service provision and reports that there was a focus on inputs or predetermined ends. Attention was on the number of beds, or day centre places, or hours of care and so on, largely irrespective of individual need. Services were interested in quantity, how much or how many, rather than quality from the perspective of service users themselves. If the service was not appropriate, disabled people could either decide to take their chances elsewhere, or to accept an inappropriate service or no service at all.

Changing services requires people to take a close look at all aspects of planning and delivery, and to be willing to alter provision should it be found wanting. Critical review and openness to change are vital as services move towards a new type of provision that places users at the centre in both planning and delivery.

Services appear to be in a state of flux. While person-centred planning has become common parlance in services that are concerned with care and support, it is not the case that it has been fully adopted or implemented across social care provision. Nevertheless changes are reported. Rose points out that a shifting philosophical position is evident. This is one that draws on the strengths of service users, treats them as responsible adults and is consistent with an ethos where users are partners.

It seems possible that, as Nolan contends, client centredness is likely to become the watchword for the twenty-first century in social care services. But progress in the implementation of person-centred planning in practice is slow. It is hampered by a number of factors including changes in culture and power relations, funding structures, infrastructure, the adequacy of staffing and staff skill base, as well as approaches to service management and staff supervision.

There is some evidence of good practice within services and improved outcomes among service users following the implementation of person-centred planning. For instance, Parley reports improvements in the opportunities available for people to make everyday choices, finding that staff were more respectful of service users, following the implementation of person-centred planning within a residential service for people with learning difficulties.

Mansell and Beadle-Brown, among others, state that systematic evidence is scant, beyond case studies showing improved outcomes following the implementation of person-centred planning.

However, Emerson and Stancliffe argue that the literature on 'positive behaviour support' and 'active support', as well as on the development of individualised services for people with high support needs, provides sufficient evidence to show that individual planning and action result in positive benefits to people with learning difficulties.

Policy Developments

Government policy recommends a collaborative and inclusive approach to service delivery within social care. In his speech to the Community Care Live conference, Stephen Ladyman (then Parliamentary Under Secretary of State for Community) announced a new 'vision' for social care, stating that services should be delivered and arranged in ways that are 'person-centred, proactive and seamless'.

Person-centred planning has been adopted as a central strand of British public policy for the development of support for people … commensurate with their needs and life or lifestyle ambitions.

It is clear that person-centred planning lies at the heart of current thinking relating to the provision of social care services. However, as far back as 1989, principles underlying person-centred planning were present in policy documents. The White Paper, Caring People: Community Care in the Next Decade and Beyond states that social and health care services should be designed 'to provide the right amount of care and support to help people to achieve maximum possible independence and ... help them achieve their full potential'. A second key concept was to 'give people a greater individual say in how they live their lives and the services they need to help them do so' (Department of Health).

The provision of individualised care is emphasised in most national policy, and for many care settings and in respect of many groups of service users.

The Essence of Care document is a patient-centred benchmarking tool for health professionals. However, it does not offer any specific benchmark to evaluate person-centred planning and the tool as a whole does not address the individual's well-being status. It focuses on aspects of physical health care such as continence and hygiene. In response, the Alzheimer's Society offers standards in person-centred care for care homes to supplement the Department of Health's Essence of Care document.

The National Service Framework for Mental Health (Department of Health) builds on The Health of the Nation key area handbook on mental illness (Department of Health). Both emphasise the need for NHS commissioners, providers and local authorities to consult with users and carers about community care planning for people with mental health problems.

In the field of learning difficulties, the White Paper Valuing People: A New Strategy for Learning Disability in the 21st Century (Department of Health) defines a context for person-centred planning that is comprehensive, systematic and challenging to current local and national practices. Lunt and Thompson state that there is an almost universal declaration of commitment to the ideal of participation, equality and social integration by service providers to people with intellectual difficulties. These are driven by policy as well as being influential on policy developments in a reciprocal manner, as the development of person-centred planning demonstrates.

The implementation of person-centred planning mandates that service providers and practitioners know people as individuals. This is consistent with policy vision across social care services, and evident in, for example, the National Service Framework for Older People, which defines care as that which 'respects people as individuals and is organised around their needs'.

Nolan et al. state that person-centred planning is an oft-quoted but ill-defined concept, which nevertheless exerts a considerable influence on policy, practice and academic literature. Definitions throughout the literature abound. What does seem wanting is evidence of widespread implementation, which would constitute a move beyond conceptualisation of ideas that remain high on the policy agenda.

The scale of the task outlined in policy is very ambitious. As discussed earlier, the complexity of implementation is not always taken into account in policy documents. Contradictions or tensions are also apparent between policy and practice documents, thus increasing difficulty in implementation. This is exemplified within the field of learning difficulties where Care Standards firmly state that no one can be supervised by someone who is untrained or who has not been checked by the Criminal Records Bureau. Alternatively, Cambridge suggests that, as brokerage services and similar expand, through Direct Payments for example, the system of person-centred planning may be a means to counter the risks of exploitation.

While policy provides direction and vision for the future of social care services, it needs to be followed by widespread changes in practice. For these to take place a revision of the infrastructure and strategic design of services is required, so as to support and facilitate the desired goal of a new style of support for service users.

Person-centred planning has become the common-sense approach to the development and delivery of social care services in the UK. There seems to be no serious alternative. However, the way that services are organised, the resources available, the funding structures, strategies for multi-agency working and the prevailing culture within services all impact on whether the implementation of person-centred planning can be achieved successfully or not.

For person-centred planning to really help change people's lives it needs to be linked to the way in which resources are allocated and used. Contemporary social care services have inherited a resource system based on a now largely discredited mode of service delivery. It is apparent therefore that in order to facilitate a new way of delivering services – that is, through person-centred planning – a change in how resources are managed and allocated is needed. Such a system change is required in relation to authorising, contracting and paying for services.

Mansell and Beadle-Brown note that resource constraints undermine the ability of service providers to turn person-centred planning into action. For instance, a lack of resources in a particular area may affect the kinds of choices that people make when devising their plans.

Staff are a key resource needed for making person-centred planning possible, both in terms of the adequacy of staffing levels and the skill base of a staff team. Mansell and Beadle-Brown warn that skill shortages can impede implementation of plans, while Packer points to a strain on resources in terms of lack of staff.

Crawford notes that staff shortages can mean standards of care are far from ideal; while Packer is concerned that it is service users who bear the brunt of staff shortages, although this is also likely to place increased stress or even despair on staff – another factor liable to impede the implementation of person-centred planning. Staff shortages may also impact on families.

Kydd states that the solution is not always in the form of increased resources in terms of more staff, but in positive teams who work together to develop appropriate working environments for person-centred planning to be implemented. He note that direct care staff need to feel that they are effective in their support role, otherwise they are likely to become frustrated and this may result in them moving on and changing jobs. Such instability in the workforce 'can ultimately compromise the successful implementation of even the best person-centred plans'. From the US, Boettcher et al., suggest staff development programes for care workers can make a positive difference to practice.

That it may require time does not appear to be part of its sales pitch.

Done well person-centred planning is a time-consuming process. However, there appears to be no calculation about the resource investment in terms of time that is needed. There is likely to be a strain on the system's resources in terms of the time required to create individual action plans for each person who uses the service.

Person-centred planning opens up opportunities that may mean that people require access to public or individualised transport. For example, people may need transport to get to and from paid or voluntary work opportunities, college courses, getting together with friends or family, or recreational and leisure activities. Lack of transport has the potential to compromise the integrity of a person-centred plan.

Funding

The implementation of person-centred planning should go hand in hand with restructuring services in terms of required funding arrangements, since funding is central to issues of control for consumers. Changes to funding arrangements need to be in terms of an assessment of funding needs based on an individual's requirements rather than a fixed level based on supposed whole-service requirements. It is restated in the Green Paper on adult social care and the Strategy for an Ageing Population. From 2006, a series of 13 local authorities embarked on this approach. If funding is linked to services rather than individuals, then the choices open to person-centred planning teams are limited to available services from existing disability service providers.

Direct Payments, where people receive money to buy their own support instead of receiving services, are a relatively recent advance. They enable people to have more choice and control over their lives, and to make decisions about their support in line with the principles of person-centred planning. But most people do not have Direct Payments and Mansell and Beadle-Brown recommend that this option be extended to more people in order to facilitate the implementation of person-centred planning – a policy goal more widely espoused (Department of Health).

Cash instead of care systems are not unique to the UK and some make more explicit links to person-centred planning. Fortune et al.

describe features of a system for funding in Wyoming, US that supports person-centred planning. This enables people to have an individual portable budget for them to use to purchase services. Another programe, In Control, has been piloted in six local authorities in the UK. This uses a resource allocation system that makes it possible for local authorities to establish how much funding is needed for each individual service user .

Strategic Targets

Felce highlights what he regards as a fundamental problem in the development of person-centred services – that is that the Government has abandoned provisional all-service targets in favour of developing services that are person centred. However, he states that 'there is no incompatibility between setting targets for populations as a whole and individual assessment of the precise nature of service input different people require or want'. One target set by *Valuing People* is for local areas to implement person-centred planning. Recommendations from the evaluation of person-centred planning include requesting that the Department of Health develops a 'clear strategic plan for supporting the development of PCP', including financial support for development activities, guidance for local authorities and the NHS, professional guidance for care managers and specialist staff, and expectations that training equips practitioners to use person-centred planning approaches.

Inter/multi-agency Working

Inter-agency or multi-agency collaboration is regarded as conducive to the realisation of person-centred plans. According to Towell and Sanderson, multi-agency engagement needs to be at three levels. First, at a personal level, the focus should be on increasing opportunities available to individuals. Second, at a service level, managers need to increase the capacity of staff to be able to deliver personalised supports. Rose cautions against the assumption that inter-agency working at a structural/managerial level equals improved outcomes for service users. However, multi-agency engagement at all three levels as discussed above may mean that collaboration actually results in positive outcomes within the person-centred paradigm.

Mainstream and Specialist Services

The literature identifies the benefits of inclusive policies on behalf of mainstream services. This means that people who have traditionally used specialist services gain access to mainstream provision. Doing this increases the options available to people, thus enabling greater choice and promoting inclusion.

To facilitate this Towell and Sanderson recommend that specialist services learn how to work with and negotiate access to mainstream services. Moreover, mainstream services may need to make adaptations so as to be able to accommodate the needs of people who have traditionally engaged only with specialist services.

Service Delivery

Person-centred planning creates opportunities for flexible support. Plans are developed collaboratively with people themselves and with their informal and formal support networks, and typically build on people's strengths, abilities, goals and desires. Principles of choice, empowerment and inclusion are fostered. However, traditional models of service delivery tend to base provision around the perceived needs of many, rather than the agreed needs of individuals.

Vital to the design of individual support packages is attention to the breadth of each person's background, experience and personal attributes.

Information necessary to the design of individual support programes is attention to:

1 History and experiences
2 Health and well-being
3 Important relationships and social contacts
4 Community life
5 Preferences
6 Rituals and routines
7 Communication strategies
8 Aspirations and fears

9 Reputation

10 Level of self-determination.

However, traditional models of service delivery tend to serve large numbers of people, and this can be a barrier to planning and delivering individualised support. For instance, overcrowding in living environments, where ten or more people share accommodation, or where people are typically in large groups in day care centres, can result in service users spending time regularly with people they don't get on with or taking part in non-preferred and standardised activities. Thus, person-centred planning is impeded by the traditional model of service delivery, and radical changes are needed so as not to compromise contemporary vision because of the inheritances of the past.

Culture

If person-centred care is going to work then it is not just about individual change but a whole culture change.

Person-centred planning represents a culture shift for most agencies. The importance of recognising the prevailing culture within services as a major factor in underpinning how services are planned and delivered is widely emphasised in the literature.

A fundamental change in the culture that governs services is a prerequisite to the successful delivery of person-centred planning. This means a realignment of power relations in the direction of service users. There are a number of strategies that would enable service users to have increased power over the service they receive.

There is a need to understand person-centred care as a life philosophy – an aspiration about being human, about pursuing the meaning of self, respecting difference, valuing equality, facing the anxieties, threats and guilt in our own lives, emphasising strengths in others and celebrating uniqueness and our own 'personhood'.

A service culture that is open to the possibilities of person-centred planning and willing to take risks and think outside of the traditional service model can enable service users to achieve the kinds of successes described above. Cultural changes are whole-service changes, affecting not just the way that services are delivered but also working practice and managerial style.

One of the greatest barriers to achieving person-centred planning is the lack of belief among frontline workers and service providers that it is a real possibility. A passionate vision, together with a thorough evaluation of belief systems that underpin practice, is needed for person-centred planning to become a reality throughout services.

Issues Relating to Service Users and Their Families

Service users are the reason why public services and support systems exist. People using services aim to live independently in an environment in which they can thrive and live life to the full. The expectations of different groups of service users may vary according to their individual needs and circumstances; people's views are not homogeneous and may change over time. This underlines the importance of services that are tailored around the needs of individuals, open to change, sensitive to the changing views of service users and able to adapt accordingly.

Scale of the Task

Mansell and Beadle-Brown state that service-wide implementation of person-centred planning within services for people with learning difficulties is 'an extremely ambitious target for public policy', if only because of the numbers of people involved and the nature of people's difficulties. While they locate their discussion in relation to learning difficulty, the points made are likely to resonate across the range of social care service users. However, it is recognised that the implementation of person-centred planning will take time. Therefore, while the task is considerable and the demands on services are growing, a steady and dedicated approach over a realistic timescale will enable widespread adoption of person-centred planning within services and for each service user. The scale of the undertaking in itself should therefore be thought of as a challenge rather than as a barrier.

Focus on Ability

While the degree of disability, illness or complexity of need should not be considered to be a barrier to achieving a person-centred approach to support for any service user, there are more complicated issues associated with more complex needs. For instance, people with a severe disability may have encountered obstacles in the development of sustainable friendships or relationships, which are regarded as central to the facilitation of person-centred planning. Therefore, the development of a network of informal support or a circle of support may be harder to instigate.

Crawford recognises the increasing involvement of users of mental health services in shaping developments in mental health practice such as person-centred planning; however, he identifies obstacles that have been encountered in achieving this.It may be the case that service users with more complex needs place a greater challenge to service providers in implementing person-centred planning.

Service Users

The legacy of services where users were considered to be passive recipients of care and were not asked about what kind of services they needed or would like has led to them often perceiving that they can achieve little in terms of influencing how services are designed or delivered.

Doris Clark and Robert Garland report their experiences and argue that circles of support are an integral part of person-centred planning. As they observe, people with learning difficulties are often not short of plans, but these are generally imposed on them. Being the 'subject' of a person-centred plan is also something that only those concerned can explain, and Robert Garland's personal account suggests that initial feelings of nervousness can be overcome, although some topics may be sensitive. Individuals want more control; families want more control; the self-advocacy movement wants people to have more control and central government sees the increasing personalisation of social care as an important goal.

Power Relations/Inclusion

It is widely recognised in the literature that, in order for person-centred planning to be achieved, a change in the culture and thinking within services is needed. Power is an issue because it is not always equally apportioned. This means that some people have more power than others and, traditionally within services, power has resided in the hands of service providers rather than service users. One legacy of this is that service users perceive that their ability to influence services is limited.

Stainton reports that social workers seem to generally recognise and accept a change in the nature of their relationships with clients, 'from one characterised more by paternalism and control to one of equality and partnership'. However, Campbell, taking a closer look, questions the reality of growing equality in power relations, where he observes service users are often invited to take part but are never involved in instigating change.

Relationship between Service Users and Staff

The relationship between service users and support staff will necessarily alter with the introduction of person-centred planning. The professional role will no longer involve the collection and storing of information about service users and the authority to make decisions about people's lives. Instead a shared process of decision making with individuals and others who care about them will be enacted.

Person-centred planning begins when people decide to listen carefully and in ways that can strengthen the voice of people who have been or are at risk of being silenced.

Positive relationships between service users and staff are needed to make person-centred planning a possibility. However, Mansell and Beadle-Brown point out that 'challenging behaviour' such as aggressive or self-injurious behaviour on the part of individuals may lead to negative emotional consequences for staff. Appropriate supervision and planning of services, perhaps through the mechanism of person-centred teams, could address difficulties such as these, so as to prevent poor relationships between staff and service users becoming a barrier to person-centred planning.

Cultural Diversity

It is important that service providers are familiar with cultural practices, religion, religious observance and language of those using their services. However, Iliffe and Manthorpe state that this should not be 'relegated to an ethnic minority agenda', but rather should be applicable to all individuals. They go on to point out that person-centred services, by virtue of the principles that govern the person-centred approach, are likely to take into account the particular needs of individuals, since the service is designed around individual circumstances and need rather than a 'one size fits all' universal service, wherein cultural needs can be inconvenient or overlooked. The need for such an approach is demonstrated by Hubert's interviews with 30 families from South Asian backgrounds who felt very unsupported, uncertain of the future and isolated from service and informal networks in the main. Shah has identified the risks of establishing specialist services to meet cultural needs and to respond to disadvantage and discrimination, and argues that such services may be short-term and hard to sustain.

Families

The role of families is central to the success of person-centred planning. La Fountaine criticises person-centred planning as too individualistic, failing to see the person within the structure of their family. By contrast, Sanderson argues that person-centred planning necessarily locates people in the context of their families and the wider community. The role of and the inclusion of nonprofessionals in the form of family and friends of service users are key components of person-centred planning. A basic challenge to working in a person-centred way lies in figuring out how best to encourage and include family members, friends and selected others to take part in the process. Families of people with dementia commonly prefer that their relative is cared for at home, where 'a little extra something' can be given. However, the strain on families can be considerable and it is recognised that they need support too; families have said that they would value confidants to talk to about the problems they face. It is important that a balance is found between involving families and ensuring that service users themselves remain at the centre of planning and delivery of their supports.

Brown with Scott warns that families and other informal networks do not always act in the best interests of disabled people, and they provide a series of examples from practice where the person-centred planning model is 'strained'.

Information for Families

Central to helping families to offer informal support within the parameters of a person-centred approach is the provision of information and training for family members. Indeed, person-centred planning strategies recommend training for families but Routledge and Gitsham note that training has been largely focused on staff to the exclusion of families and service users. However, Sanderson reports that this is changing and that, although many training courses have been held for support staff, there are increasing numbers for families, advocates and self-advocates.

Relationship between Staff and Families

Families and professionals may have different ideas about what constitutes best support. However, Sanderson argues that service providers should view families positively. She states that the family understands the person from its own perspective and there is a need for service providers to make a concerted effort to develop relationships with families. Stereotyping families as either 'overprotective' or 'disinterested' is detrimental to the person-centred planning process.

Issues Specific to Particular Populations

(i) People with Learning Difficulties

(a) Communication

There is a common over-reliance on verbal communication and staff can often misjudge how much or how little service users understand. Imaginative means of communication can be developed in respect of the needs and abilities of individuals. Dick and Purvis outline how one county's total communication plan became one of the main footings for the person-centred approaches. They report an example of work with one individual, John, to illustrate ways in which communications can help in the building of a plan, to enable it to be reviewed, to share information and to assess the impact or outcome of a more person-centred approach on his life. In the absence of attention to communication, there is a risk of a lack of understanding between users and service providers – a clear impediment to person-centred planning.

(b) Expectations

People often have low expectations of what is possible for people with learning difficulties; this can impact on the options that are available.

(c) Choice

For many people with learning difficulties the concept of choice is oblique. Some may have spent much of their lives in long-stay hospitals, have taken no role in decisions that affect their lives and need a great deal of support to understand what it means to make a choice.

(ii) People with Dementia

Ericson et al. state that it is beneficial for people with dementia to develop relationships with a small number of individuals. They go on to show that care staff can help people with dementia to retain personhood. Assisting people to maintain their individuality in spite of their disability is important in person-centred care. This involves an awareness of the individual's life before dementia, so as to be able to understand the individual in his or her own biographical context.

(iii) People with Mental Health Problems

Barriers to inclusion and person-centred planning for people with mental health problems are negative social attitudes towards them. Concerns about public fears of people with mental illness seem to take precedence over their quality of care.

Perspective of Frontline Staff

An important goal of most service providers is to enable a good quality of life for service users. The role of frontline workers is central to the realisation of services that are based around person-centred planning. The needs and views of frontline workers must be taken into account in order for services to succeed in its implementation.

The way a service is managed directly affects the ability of frontline workers to perform their job well and to promote independent living through person-centred planning. Frontline workers are faced with obstacles that sometimes prevent them from providing what people would prefer.

Staff Abilities

Mansell and Beadle-Brown identify a skill deficit among many frontline workers, mainly due to limited training for staff. They point to evidence that shows that staff working with people with learning difficulties, particularly those with more complex needs, typically offer little support for people to engage in meaningful activities in their home life or in the wider community. Consequently, people frequently have restricted social networks. This may result in obstacles to further engagement in the community or in the construction of a circle of support to help facilitate person-centred planning. This is identified as a potential barrier to the implementation of person-centred planning. Limited skills among care staff may engender further difficulties in implementing person-centred planning.

However, while training staff to acquire the skills to implement new ways of working is central, it is also important that existing skills and abilities are recognised, acknowledged and built on. Acknowledging this and recognising it as a key skill in producing plans and actions that are person-centred provides a foundation for staff to develop their practice and is potentially a confidence boost in their ability to acquire other skills needed to implement person-centred planning. Additionally, staff may have interests or skills developed outside their working lives.

Staff often know what they would like to do, but lack the confidence, time or resources to put this into action. From interviews with care staff working in a residential home for people with dementia some staff appear to be what Sheard terms 'naturals', in that they had an instinctive understanding of what it is to adopt a person-centred approach to care.

Staff who are 'naturals' are 'people who instinctively live their lives with the ability to connect to another's feelings, who use their instincts and gut feelings, who feel person centred care rather than just practise it. They work with their heart rather than their mind'. The contention is that they then stand a better chance of making their points heard and not being overridden by staff who may be more highly qualified, but who may nevertheless be attached to outdated beliefs and modes of practice.

Training

When we consider all that is involved in giving person-centred care, it is clear that it is unrealistic to expect staff to work in this way if we do not equip them with the necessary skills, facilitate the development of their insight and help them to build on the valuable resources they bring to care-giving.

The literature identifies a significant lack of training for frontline staff in working with person-centred planning. Sheard notes that there is no continuous learning culture within many services, and argues that staff need training that will empower them and encourage them to be proud of their work and to recognise the value of the knowledge they already possess.

Loveday states that training should address the 'new culture' and provide time for staff to re-evaluate existing attitudes and practices in line with a person-centred method. This is considered to be an opportunity for staff to reflect on their practice and challenge themselves to consider new approaches. A person-centred approach to training should be taken, as this would enable staff to understand the concept through direct experience.

The training deficit among social care staff has been acknowledged in recent government initiatives, which endorse attempts to increase training opportunities. Ray makes recommendations regarding the manner in which training is carried out. In their view training should:

— Be interesting and informative
— Be helpful in unpicking difficult practice issues and concepts in person-centred planning
— Take a straightforward, jargon-free approach
— Be interactive and flexible in use.

Likewise, Mansell and Beadle-Brown argue that training should focus on action and on facilitating change rather than just planning.

Culture – staff Attitudes

The need for a culture change within services to facilitate the implementation of person-centred planning is a theme running through much of the literature. The culture of a service can be regarded as bringing together the underlying guiding principles that govern the way in which it is run and how support is delivered.

Loveday, discussing services for people with dementia, points out that staff have considerable power and influence over the well-being of service users. She contends that they are often tied to old ways of thinking, but notes that this is not their fault, rather it is a priority of training to challenge the thinking that informs practice. Changes in thinking require a rethinking of power relations, so that power can be vested in individual service users, thus enabling choice and the potential for inclusion and self-determination. Person-centred planning is based on a completely different way of seeing and working with people ... which is fundamentally about sharing power and community inclusion.

Role of Managers

Managers have a significant role to play in enabling staff teams to adopt a person-centred approach. Sanderson advocates that service managers extend the principles of person-centred planning to their staff teams, in order to develop what she describes as person-centred teams. This would require a change of thinking on the part of managers.

Table 1. Characteristics of person-centred team leaders and person-centred teams

Characteristics of effective person -centred team leaders	Characteristics of a person-centred team
See themselves as coaches who bring out the best in people.	Sees the team's purpose as supporting people to achieve the lifestyle they want

Demonstrate and articulate the values of the organisation.	and contributing to their community.
Look for ways to use staff's interests and strengths in directly supporting people.	Highly values personal commitment and relationships with the people it supports.
Share decision making.	Reviews itself, not the people it supports.
Have a clear vision and direction.	Invests in community connections.
Encourage personal involvement with the people being supported.	Continually tries new ideas and evaluates whether they improve the support it is providing to achieve the team's purpose.

Research confirms that frontline workers often lack opportunities for involvement in care planning or other decision-making activities, which may compound their difficulties in providing adequate support to promote independent living.

Staff state that they are often unsure what managers expect from them and find it difficult to separate person-centred planning from previous planning initiatives.

Uncertainty, adherence to a chain of command, maintaining a 'professional distance' from service users and a depleted sense of value in the role carried out by frontline workers all stand at odds with the characteristics that Sanderson describes as essential components of person-centred teams.

Support for Staff

Killick and Allan emphasise the importance of support for frontline staff in what is often a difficult and demanding role. Descriptions of a number of informal support structures, outside of managerial or agency supervision, are emerging from the literature. Many of them are commended by practitioners themselves as useful support mechanisms. They include the following.

1 Working with other staff teams in a consortium to share problems and discuss solutions; this, it is suggested, will increase confidence and improve practice.

2 Staff may experience the work to be emotionally demanding and suggest the development of networks to support them in their work with people with dementia.

3 Staff mentoring may help staff understand different approaches to their work.

Personal Dilemmas

Surrendering control over what happens in someone's life is difficult for many professionals when the choices that a person makes are at odds with the choices and expectations of professionals. Choices that people make may conflict with professional training, duties of care, or personal beliefs of staff.

New Initiatives

In Control is a programe that aims to guide local authorities in altering their entire service system towards self-directed support. It is currently being piloted in six local authorities in the UK and is focused primarily on people with learning difficulties. However, it is intended that the model will eventually be extended across the range of social care services.

In Control has developed five ideas that, it is hoped, will facilitate the goal of greater control by service users in the planning of their support. Each idea is described below.

1 *Fair entitlements:* this involves a system whereby resources are allocated in such a way that local authorities are able to assess the amounts needed for each individual service user, thus enabling more effective financial planning and greater potential in the design of individualised services.
2 *Supported decisions*: people may need help in making decisions. This may be in the form of a proxy. Systems for decision making should be regularly reviewed; the default position should not automatically be that professionals take decisions *for* service users.
3 *Assuming capacity:* the programe acts on the assumption that people have the capacity to take decisions on how they want to live and to organise the support they need.
4 *Support brokerage:* people are likely to need help to make plans and implement them. Much of this help can be found outside formal support networks.

5 *Contractual freedom*: people should have real control in how they use their resources. It is inappropriate for people to be tied into the use of particular services.

In Control is founded on the belief that people with disabilities should not be defined by social care organisations they use or by the parameters of the condition they have, but that they should be seen as a full citizen by right. Duffy has produced a model of 'six keys to citizenship'. These include: self-determination, direction, money, a home, support and community life. Some people will need help to achieve some or all of these aspects of citizenship.

Support Time and Recovery workers

The Support Time and Recovery (STR) Worker programe is a new public health initiative in the field of mental health. This national programe was instigated by the Department of Health in November 2003, with the aim of creating 3,000 Support Time and Recovery Workers by 2006. The STR worker is a member of a team that provides mental health services and who focuses directly on the needs of service users. The values that inform the work of STR workers centre on meeting the needs of service users by paying attention to and respecting their wishes to lead as ordinary a life as possible. STR workers help service users to have an ordinary life, facilitating their recovery by assisting with everyday, practical needs in whatever setting they find themselves. STR workers are being appointed with a view to the improvement of services for people with mental health problems. Benefits may be to the individual and their carers, but also to the service, in terms of job satisfaction, and recruitment and retention of frontline workers in the mental health teams where STR workers are based.

The role of the STR Worker is outlined in the Department of Health guidance document. In brief, this includes working to promote independent living, provide companionship, offer practical support, help people to gain access to resources, provide information on health promotion, identify early signs of relapse and support service users to participate in their treatment. STR workers are not involved in clinical decisions, medical treatment or therapeutic counselling. They adopt an inclusive, sensitive, creative and empowering attitude to their role, and work within the bounds of confidentiality and nondiscriminatory practice. The STR Worker programe is currently being piloted in 19 sites across the country. One of these is East Suffolk Mind, which reports that one role of the Support Time Recovery worker is to promote the idea that people can recover from a mental health problem.

This person-centred approach to the support of people with mental health problems is in its early stages, but indications are that service users are greeting it as a welcome addition to mental health services. Widespread implementation of this strategy may prove if it is providing and resourcing a person-centred service for users of mental health social care services. The evaluation focused on three pilot sites – two in the North of England and one in London – and drew on the views of service users (n = 16), as well as staff within the mental health team, including STR workers (n = 21 – more than half of those employed at the time), other front-line staff and managers (n = 24). The findings showed a very positive response to the STR worker, although some other team members did not understand the role, showing that induction of other team members is important. The involvement of service users in the process of recruitment and so on, and as workers, is a positive feature. Service users appreciate the time spent with them, although some wanted more. The nature of the relationship between the service user and worker was a key to success promoting social inclusion and recovery. STR workers had better role clarity than community mental health nurses and social workers. Working within plans for recovery, this type of work may help translate person-centred planning into action for people with mental health problems who are not so commonly considered in the literature on person-centred planning.

What Works in Person-centred Planning

The two initiatives described above demonstrate how the principles of person-centred planning can be carried forward into action. A fundamental problem that emerges from the literature is that, while ideas of person-centred planning abound and the principles are widely applauded and endorsed, there appears to be a hiatus between this and implementation.

It is clear that several factors need to be in place to make person-centred planning work. These include: adherence to the underlying principles of person-centred planning; sufficient resources and appropriate funding; and a trained, confident and well-equipped staff team who are managed in an inclusive and empowering style, which institutes clear planning and direction for the future. Achieving person-centred planning is not a rapid process and it is important that sufficient time is taken for initiatives to be put in place before policy makers, practitioners and users become tired of waiting and new policy initiatives emerge.

Many of the barriers we identify confirm those specified by Kinsella, such as a lack of evidence for person-centred planning, the perceived complexity of the process, the risk of the process becoming tokenistic, the search for the 'best' type of plan, the reliance on the very staff and services to implement a plan that may make them redundant, and a lack of support among some key stakeholders, such as advocacy organisations and some families. However, this overview of the literature does suggest some key developments have take place since the start of the millennium.

References

Lillrank, A. (2003) 'Back Pain and the Resolution of Diagnostic Uncertainty in Illness Narratives', *Social Science and Medicine* 57(6): 1045–54.

Maxwell, J. A. (1992) 'Understanding and Validity in Qualitative Research', *Harvard Educational Review* 62(3): 279–300.

Mishler, E. G. (1995) 'Models of Narrative Analysis: A Typology', *Journal of Narrative and Life History* 5(2): 87–123.

Riessman, C. K. (ed.) (1994) *Qualitative Studies in Social Work Research.* Thousand Oaks, CA: Sage.

9

Social Work and the Ethics of Care

Recent years have witnessed a major reassessment of the nature, focus and organisation of social work and social care services in much of the English speaking Western world. In England, under the auspices of a New Labour government, this has been taking place under the rationale of 'modernising' public services. In many respects the modernisation agenda can be seen as a reaction against the inflexibility, inefficiency and aloofness of both large stage bureaucracies and the professionals who play key roles in the delivery of services. The visions for the future are articulated in the language of community and citizenship, reciprocity and responsibility, justice and fairness, partnership and participation, and crucially recognise that a variety of state, voluntary and informal services provide vital contributions to the care and support of individuals and thus the health of society more generally.

At the same time the way in which such changes have been introduced has very much been of a top-down nature. More particularly, the process of modernisation can be seen as furthering the growing managerialisation of social work and social care via its intense focus on performance and efficiency targets, together with the growing emphasis of centralised and formulaic regimes of inspection and scrutiny.

In recent years, governments have imposed and refined systems of audit and new operational and administrative procedures. Social work practice has become more legalised, and notions of 'evidence-based practice' have become pervasive. These developments, which emphasise practitioner accountability to stakeholders other than clients, seem to dominate the nature of what it is to be a practitioner, particularly in the public sector. Social workers are required to take a more instrumental and impersonal approach to their work, and perceive that care for service users is little more than labour in the service of economy, efficiency, and effectiveness.

Recent years have also witnessed the publication of a number of texts which have attempted to develop perspectives which are explicitly critical and reflexive and which, to varying degrees, draw upon insights offered by a number of postmodern perspectives. Partly drawing on Peter Leonard, Jan Fook and Karen Healy see the essential elements of these emerging critical social work approaches as emphasising a: commitment to standing alongside oppressed and impoverished populations; the importance of dialogic relations between workers and service users; the significance of social, economic, and political systems in shaping individual experiences and social relationships, including interactions within the practice context; an orientation towards the transformation of processes and structures that perpetuate domination and exploitation, and thus emphasises the importance of social justice and equality.

Beyond this it seems that discussions of care within the critical social work literature, until very recently, have been remarkable only by their absence, such that it has seemed there has almost been an assumption that social work is so tainted by its associations with care that the word should be expunged both from its lexicon and rationale. In our view this is unfortunate. Not only has the notion of care been at the core of social work values, theory and practice since its inception but it is the central part of our argument that its rehabilitation can provide a key counterweight to the increasing processes of managerialisation which seem so pervasive.

That social work practitioners value care, and perceive that their desire to prioritise it in their practice is not shared by government funders is illustrated for us in a recent study comparing practitioners' perceptions of their own and their funding department's priorities in non-government family support services. Experienced family support practitioners were offered a list of eight characteristics from which to choose those they considered to be the three most important characteristics of effective services. Practitioners perceived that the funding department's top priority was the legally oriented characteristic that 'the service complies with legal obligations, such as child protection legislation', with 91 per cent of practitioners including this in their list of the department's top three. Whereas 44 per cent of practitioners included the characteristic 'workers are compassionate and caring' among their top three, only five per cent perceived it to be a priority for the Department.

At the same time, we are aware that the early years of the new millennium have witnessed the publication of a number of texts which have underlined the importance for social work and social care of seriously engaging with feminist thinking about the 'ethics of care'. It is our view that such developments provide us with a real possibility for not just rehabilitating the notion of care to the centre of social work but in a way which contributes to and builds on the arguments developed within the critical social work literature. Of particular importance is the capacity of the discourse of the ethics of care to offer ways of conceiving and representing those aspects of social work which are obscured by the rational technical focus of the managerialism that has come to dominate the way social work and social care is increasingly thought about, organised and practised.

Rationalisation of Social Work

While religious convictions about the nature of human struggles shaped social work during its development in the latter part of the nineteenth century, the twentieth century saw increasing attempts to professionalise the role. The main protagonists aspired to mimic the traditional professions, particularly medicine, but at no time has social work achieved this level of authority, status or legitimacy.

As models of organisation, decision-making, and practice, professionalism and bureaucracy, have shaped social workers' capacity to enact care. One way of seeing the 'problem' these approaches pose for the theory and practice of social work is to look through the lens of gender. If we see masculinity and femininity not as attributes of individuals in any essentialist sense but as cultural representations.

As a normative cultural project, masculinity entails separation from others, the creation of a strongly bounded sense of self, an emphasis on individuality, a wish for power, agency and action, and for being a subject—making a difference in the world; whereas femininity involves a continuing experience of connection with others, a focus on interdependence, and a sense of self in relation to others, rather than as always autonomous and apart. Masculinity is crucially concerned with establishing relations of domination and ensuring their stability and predictability. Autonomous, controlled individuals are brought into ordinary relations with each other in pursuit of agreed goals. Emotions, enthusiasms, and vulnerabilities are seen to be an impediment.

In its ideal typical form, the bureaucratic approach emphasises formality and distance as the only routes to rational decision making. The impartiality of the decision, the impersonality of the bureaucrat, and the unequivocal authority of its hierarchy are the key characteristics of bureaucracy. Masculinity's version of rational action conceives itself as autonomous and independent of the other. The impartiality, impersonality, formality, and distance characterising the ideal typical bureaucracy reflect these masculine cultural characteristics.

In apparent contrast, the ideal typical professional appears to have all of the flexibility that the rule and hierarchy bound bureaucrat lacks. The true professional acts autonomously, refers difficult cases to a more experienced colleague, and is not required to bow to hierarchy as the bureaucrat would be. However, as Celia Davies has argued, while bureaucratic and professional approaches may seem at first sight diametrically opposed, on closer inspection the notion of the professional is similarly gendered masculine. Again, there is a strong element of the need for distance and impersonality. Expertise derives from formal training, which is itself based on rational science. Perhaps most crucially, autonomy stands at the very heart of traditional concepts of the professional.

In many respects, therefore, and as Davies argues, the ideal types of the professional and the bureaucratic forms of practice and organisation share much. Both are oriented to control and mastery; to establish order through implementation of an abstract decision set of processes. Both rely on hierarchical relations and promote distance from their clienteles. Both the bureaucrat and the professional are invested with an authority for decision making as if they inhabit a sovereign court, where their decisions are rarely questioned, and where those on the receiving end are grateful.

Social work has never had this kind and level of authority and power. The designation 'bureau-profession' is simply one sign of its failure to achieve full professional status. More particularly, the nature of social work, particularly its engagement with the most marginalised and deprived members of society, meant that it had difficulty in fulfilling the characteristics required to fulfil this status.

More recent years have seen an important shift in its trajectory of development. The alleged failures and problems of social work that became apparent in a series of child abuse tragedies and public inquiries during the 1970s and 1980s prefigured the increasing criticisms of most health and welfare professional occupations that emerged in the political and public arenas during the 1990s. Both the bureaucratic and professional approaches to health and welfare which became so dominant in the post-war period were seen to be wanting. Simultaneously, there occurred increasing questioning of the welfare state and the growth of a new approach to health and welfare which placed the notion of managerialism at its centre.

This context of failure has provided the key ideological impetus for criticising and trying to move beyond the models of both the bureaucracy and the profession which were central to the way health and welfare services were thought about and organised in the second half of the twentieth century. Governments have sought to remedy this failure with a new governance model: managerialism, often referred to as the 'new public management'.

From the managerialist perspective, professionals and bureaucrats are self interested and untrustworthy. Both need to be 'managed' by new mechanisms that establish clear lines and criteria of accountability, to restore the integrity of and community trust in public services. Amongst other innovations, managerialist governments have developed and implemented a variety of practices designed to monitor, assess, and regulate the performance of both organisations and workers delivering public services, and those in receipt of them. These practices and their supporting ideas aim to promote a cost-conscious performance culture.

Proponents claim that these innovations remedy the problems of the old bureaucratic or professionalised approaches. However, importantly for our argument, the social relations managerialism represents and aims to institutionalise have many of the masculine characteristics already discussed. Like the bureaucrat and the professional, the ideal new manager remains distant and controlled. He takes a critical stance towards the arguments presented and the established practices of others, drawing his own conclusions based on designated general decision rules, rather than being swayed by sympathy to particular cases. Managerialism seems to celebrate critique, distance, and the ability to make difficult decisions, such that there is no attempt to hide potential hostility and warring in the way professional and bureaucratic approaches might have.

Gender and Moral Knowledge

In the early 1980s, feminist philosophers and political theorists began to overcome their historical uneasiness about engaging in debates about morality and ethics, to develop an explicitly gender-sensitive approach to moral inquiry. Perhaps the most significant product of feminism's engagement with moral philosophy has been the discourse of the ethics of care. In the ensuing twenty years, debate about the ethics of care has itself burgeoned. Our purpose here is not to provide a detailed exposition of the evolution of the discourse of the ethics of care or to account for the emergence of different strands.

The shared assumptions of the ethics of care are a set of interwoven arguments about the nature of the good in human interactions, and of how moral subjects generate and act on knowledge about the good. First among these shared assumptions of care ethics is what Selma Sevenhuijsen calls a 'relational ontology': the ethics of care places at the centre of moral inquiry the interdependence of humans and their responsibilities to each other, rather than individuals and their rights. Second, the ethics of care recognises the equal moral worth of all persons, and holds that their informal and interpersonal relations are an appropriate object and ground of moral deliberation. Third, the ethics of care emphasises caring as moral posture or disposition: moral subjects should attend to others with compassion, responding to each person as unique and irreplaceable, and recognising each moral decision as taking place within a specific context. Fourth, the nurturing at the heart of care ethics requires that caring is also a process that fosters the growth of those participating in caring relationships, and their willingness to take on open-ended responsibilities in regard to each other.

The emphasis on caring as a disposition and a process has several corollaries. From the perspective of care ethics, certain emotions, particularly empathy and compassion, are not fetters on clear and objective moral judgement, but rather are fundamental to the development of moral understanding itself. Moreover, if a moral subject is to attend to another in their concrete specificity moral decision-making will require much more than the application of principles. Feelings, the capacity to recognise 'the separate consciousness of another making its own sense of the world', and communication are all required.

Although theorists of the ethics of care agree on these matters of substance and method in moral reasoning, there remain several significant, well-recognised, and related points of contention. It is worth exploring different views on these issues among theorists of care ethics, because different constructions of these aspects of care ethics pose different opportunities and risks for social work.

Some theorists of care ethics such as Nel Noddings construct an avowedly 'feminine' ethic of care in explicit opposition to rights-based ethics. Noddings, Sara Ruddick, Virginia Held, and other influential early contributors to the discourse of the ethics of care were motivated to counter the at best patronising, at worst entirely dismissive way women and the feminine had been treated in conventional ethical inquiry. Nel Noddings, for example, in a web of arguments about gender, human nature, and moral obligation, constructs a naturalistic and expressly anti-rule and anti-political ethics of care. The central role of the mother-child relation, and her observations about gender differences in approaches to moral problems prompt Noddings to call her ethic of care a 'feminine ethic'. Although she does not 'imply a claim for all women or ... exclude men' from her ethics of care, Noddings does argue that 'there is reason to believe that women are somewhat better equipped for caring than men are'. Thus the ethics of care are tied, in this formulation, to femininity and women's experience of the private sphere.

Noddings's account is naturalistic because she links the development of a 'moral imperative' to care to what she sees as an innate 'impulse to act on behalf of the present other'. This innate impulse is fostered into the capacity for moral awareness and judgement by a cycle of caring relationships that starts with the natural care a mother gives a child. However, she continues: we are not compelled by this impulse. We have a choice; we may accept what we feel, or we may reject it. If we have a strong desire to be moral, we will not reject it, and this strong desire to be moral is derived, reflectively, from the more fundamental and natural desire to be and to remain related.

When we are faced with moral decisions about how to act as 'one-caring', Noddings argues that reference to moral principles can be a positive barrier to care; hence our designation 'anti-rule'. Discussing moral conduct by exploring language and reasoning, she contends, takes us away from an assessment of the concrete events in which we must choose whether and how to behave morally.

Constructing the scope of moral action in this way emphasises the local and contingent, placing a strong imperative on moral agents to engage practically with our fellow human beings in very day-to-day ways.

Other feminist theorists of the ethic of care take issue with approaches like Noddings's, which emphasise the role of natural care and the mother-child relationship, suspect reasoning and rules in moral inquiry, and narrowly circumscribe the limits on the obligation to care to personal relationships. Instead, more recent contributions by Selma Sevenhuijsen and Joan Tronto to the discourse of the ethics of care have emphasised the need to move beyond oppositional thinking in debates about feminist ethics, to 'denaturalise' the ethics of care, and to integrate thinking about the ethics of care with political theory and activity on a much broader stage than interpersonal relationships.

Again, the metaphor of a web is useful to capture the key arguments and their relationships. Much that distinguishes the contributions of these theorists ramifies from their position that care is necessarily a political as well as a moral concept, such that power and difference are central. Rather, at the 'macro' level of society as whole, and at the 'micro' level of interpersonal relationships, the 'politicised' approach to the ethics of care explores how the ethics of care both can illuminate problems of power and difference in existing social arrangements, and can help overcome some of the characteristic problems and dilemmas of care that unequal power engenders.

At the macro level, answers to these questions explore how class, gender, ability and race interact to distribute both the getting and giving of care. Typically, the powerful 'are more often in a position to receive or demand care than to provide it', while those with less power often find themselves 'in situations in which they provide care without much power over the conditions and the means, and often in positions of invisibility and voicelessness'.

This recognition also allows these theorists to shed light on the 'dark side' of care at the micro level. Tronto highlights two dangers of care': paternalism/ maternalism.

Parochialism results from care when we see the caring relationships in which we are engaged, and which we know best as the most important. Here Tronto highlights the particular hazard of the use of the mother child relationship as the founding metaphor of the ethics of care.

However, Tronto and Sevenhuijsen argue that a political approach to the ethics of care also offers remedies for these problems of care. In a similar vein, the emphasis on what Walker, cited above, called 'shared processes of discovery, expression, interpretation, and adjustment between persons' reflects the democratic impulse of the ethics of care.

Finally, in addition to linking caring to critiques of current social structures, and to new ways of thinking about negotiating power, privilege, and difference, politicised constructions of the ethics of care do not reject rights and justice as categories of moral and political discourse.

Opportunities and Risks

Engagement between social work and the ethics of care involves both opportunities and risks for both social workers and service users. Many social workers would recognise their working relationships with service users either in reality or in aspiration in the descriptions of the nature of moral response and action offered in the discourses of the ethics of care. The insights of the ethics of care support and articulate social workers' self-understanding as moral agents in caring relationships with service users. This has implications for the recognition of the value and efficacy of social work both in service management and wider social contexts, including current attempts to 'modernise'. As an account of decision-making in interpersonal interactions, the ethics of care also provides a gender-sensitive, moral ground to concepts of reflective practice to develop further existing alternatives to rational-technical models. Thus, the ethics of care offers social work theory and practice what might be called an 'epistemological' opportunity. In describing interactions as 'shared processes of discovery, expression, interpretation, and adjustment between persons', the ethics of care also supports social work's commitment to dialogic relations between social workers and service users.

However, despite the 'opportunities' described above, it is probably not a coincidence that the notion of care has received little recent attention in social work. As the quotation from Healy in our introduction illustrated, the critical social work literature comes close to identifying care with oppression. Care is also associated with charity for which those on the receiving end should be grateful. More recently, service user activism and social work discourses have emphasised the importance of user involvement, partnership, participation, rights, and, perhaps most significantly, empowerment. The contemporary use of the term 'service user' as opposed to 'client' symbolises this change in emphasis. To suggest that social work should look afresh at ideas about care, even in the context of debates about the ethics of care, could be seen as at best naive and at worst dangerous. Not only might it have the unintended consequence of reinforcing the existing prejudices and problems arising from the cultural and political devaluation of the feminine in a context where caring work is female dominated, but it may deflect attention from what service user movements say they want.

Focusing on the disability movement, Fiona Williams has recently explored some challenging critiques of the ethics of care that focus on the risks of conceptualising service interactions as care from a service user perspective. First, she notes that rejecting care, Wood argues for empowerment particularly where it emphasises choice and control, while Finkelstein argues that care is now so laden it should be replaced by support. Secondly, Williams points out that while the ethics of care emphasises interdependence and the relational, 'disabled people have argued for the strategic centrality of independence, tying it to the practical demand for independent living in which autonomy and control over one's life are key'. Thirdly, she considers Silvers's argument that to propose that the mutuality and closeness of family life become the paradigm in social life fails to grasp how the power inherent in extra-familial care relationships is not attenuated by the tenderness of intimacy.

These critics are responding to what Tronto identifies as the 'dark side' of care. However, we agree with Williams that service user critiques of the ethics of care share more common ground with the views they seem to oppose than may first appear, particularly when the diversity of positions within the ethics of care debate is taken into account. As proponents of the ethics of care suggest, 'we can in practice be carers or cared-for in different situations and do not always occupy one single position in this binary'. Further, both the ethics of care approach, as elaborated by Tronto and Sevenhuijsen, and the empowerment approach, as elaborated by writers like Beresford, operate within an equality paradigm.

Williams also points out that despite different emphases in their understandings of autonomy/independence, writers from within the disability movement and proponents of the politicised ethics of care both make the important distinction between the inadequate conceptualisation of autonomy as self-sufficiency, and autonomy/independence as the capacity to have choice and control over one's life. Williams herself argues that the concept of interdependence, which is so central to the ethics of care, needs to recognise that recent collective struggles around care place a premium on independence.

Finally, Williams explores how the issue of professional versus nonprofessional paid care for disabled people exposes another risk and opportunity of the ethics of care. Rather than seek the putatively unsullied care of untrained carers, Williams argues that the skills of care should be claimed as skills, 'and that the issue is how to develop training so that the knowledge and experience of disabled people and other service users influence work practices'.

Work in the UK by the National Institute for Social Work and Peter Beresford and his colleagues in this context is very instructive. As part of the debate on the future of social work in England, social work practitioners, people whose primary responsibility was to work with and be in close contact with service users themselves, came together to identify what was seen as the key characteristics of best social work practice. There was considerable overlap and consistency in terms of: a holistic approach to social and personal problem solving; a relationship based on respect; attention to the experience of individuals, groups, and communities and to their expertise, culture, and religion; recognition that the process and the relationship is part of what determines a good outcome for service users; access to independent information on which to think through options and reach decisions; service users retaining as much control as possible over their lives and the choices they make.

While debate about the ethics of care has been significantly informed by fundamental criticisms of the individualised liberal ethics of rights, it is our view that, in drawing on the politicised variant of the ethics of care, it is not helpful to see approaches based on rights/empowerment in such stark antithesis to those based on care. As Orme has recently argued, drawing on Gilligan, Jagger and Hekman, justice and care are logically compatible and indispensable to each other, and that a dialogical approach challenges binaries not only of the carer/cared for, the public/private, but that between care and justice and rights.

It is in this spirit that we feel the ethics of care provide a key critical framework for both analysing and moving beyond the current dominance of the managerialist approaches to social work. In doing so not only are we more able to see the central relevance of grappling with care theoretically and practically, but the attempts to 'modernise' will themselves have a greater chance to deliver on a range of key objectives and principles which are currently in danger of being lost. The aim to overcome the divide between rationality and the emotions in much moral, political, and epistemological thought can prove productive in the current climate.

References

Davies, H., Nutley, S. M., & Smith, P. C. (2000). *What works? Evidence-based policy in public services*. Toronto, Canada: University of Toronto Press.

DeRubeis, R. J., & Crits-Christoph, P. (1998). Empirically supported individual and group psychological treatments for adult mental disorders. *Journal of Consulting and Clinical Psychology, 66*, 37-52.

Evidence-Based MedicineWorking Group. (1992). Evidence-based medicine: A new approach to teaching the practice of medicine. *Journal of the American Medical Association, 268*, 2420-2425.

Fischer, J. (1976). *Effectiveness of social casework*. Springfield, IL: Charles C Thomas.

Foa, E. B., Keane, T. M., & Friedman, M. J. (2000). *Effective treatments for PTSD: Practice guidelines fromthe International Society for Traumatic Stress Studies*.NewYork: Guilford.

10

Challenges of Social Work

Social work takes place within a framework of law and regulation. Wherever possible, social workers aim to work in partnership with the people they are helping, encouraging them to keep control of their lives, express their views and participate in decisions that affect them. Relationships and trust are important. Sometimes however, they need the ability to stand back, make judgements and reach hard decisions in order to protect vulnerable people or to exercise control. In local authority social work, regulations often prescribe procedures for assessment, investigation and joint working with allied disciplines.

People are generally keen to manage their own affairs with a minimum of interference. Many prefer to assess their own needs and organise their own support. This is changing the way some social work tasks are defined. Much day-to-day social work has a clear preventative role, supporting parents and carers, reducing the risks of abuse and neglect, preventing family breakdown, and helping people maintain or recover their independence. Skilled social work often avoids the need for compulsory action, and enables children or adults to remain safely in their homes. Social work also works with health, education, housing and other agencies, helping people achieve joined-up solutions as well as making best use of public funds. A core task of social work is the development of working partnerships with other professionals and agencies.

To perform at their best, social workers require active support from government, employers and the public. Many social work roles help implement government policy and are essential in enabling local councils, schools and the justice services to carry out their roles. Government is responsible for ensuring resources are sufficient to meet needs and maintain standards of good practice. Local authority members and the media need help to understand the risks social workers have to manage and the high levels of responsibility they carry.

DEFINING SOCIAL WORK ROLES

Social work is practised worldwide. The following is a widely accepted international definition:

> "The social work profession promotes social change, problem solving in human relationships and the empowerment and liberation of people to enhance well-being. Utilising theories of human behaviour and social systems, social work intervenes at the points where people interact with their environments. Principles of human rights and social justice are fundamental to social work"

In preparing this Statement, the project team and Reference Group found it necessary to consider and seek answers to several different but related questions implied in the remit:

— What range of roles and tasks does modern social work encompass?

— What is unique or distinctive about social work roles and tasks compared with those of other disciplines?

— What roles and tasks require the levels of knowledge and skill possessed by social workers, as distinct from other social care staff?

— What roles and tasks should be performed only by social workers?

The Statement distinguishes "roles", based on the broad purposes of social work and the outcomes it enables people to achieve, from "tasks", the activities required to deliver those purposes and outcomes. The roles tend to be particular to social work, although they are often performed within multi-disciplinary teams and settings.

In recent years there has been a trend, reinforced by government policy, towards blurring role differences and loosening boundaries between professional disciplines. Unduly rigid boundaries are thought to cause problems to people trying to find their way round the system, and to make for inefficiency in the use of professional resources. Social work roles tend to be more elastic than those of many other disciplines, for a variety of reasons:

— Social work has to take account of people's needs, circumstances and relationships as a whole, rather than focusing on a particular condition or delivering a defined service.
— Increasingly, social workers are working in partnership with people to co-produce solutions matched to their strengths and preferences, and jointly securing the best possible outcomes.
— In enabling people to exercise control and choice, social work must respond to demands for more personalised solutions, to be flexible in finding new ways of working. and adapt to people's changing situations
— Social work as a profession plays a key role in mediating between the individual and the state, and determining when it is necessary for the state to intervene in the lives of individuals and families.
— Social work's remit for negotiating with other agencies, and coordinating support from various sources, often takes it into the territory of other services and professions.
— In helping people excluded by other services, it can be difficult for social work to draw hard and fast boundaries round its roles.
— Social work is an evolving profession, constantly responding to new policy aspirations, expanding knowledge and rising public expectations

What makes social work roles distinctive is the combination of several features. These features are considered under the following headings:

— The characteristic situations of people who receive social work support or intervention
— The functions for which social work skill and expertise are required;
— The types of outcomes social work enables people to achieve;
— The combination of knowledge, values and skills it possesses;
— The evidence base for social work practice;

— The methods and approaches it applies to assess, record and respond to people's rights and needs.

SOCIAL WORK SUPPORT OR INTERVENTION

Social work helps children, adults, families and communities in a wide variety of circumstances. It often works with people at times of crisis, or in situations where other services have been unable or unwilling to help. Social work applies expert knowledge and skills to analyse complex individual, family and social situations where there is a need to assess high levels of risk and uncertainty, conflicting interests and difficult choices, to make judgements and to take action appropriately.

Social workers characteristically find themselves in lead roles where:

— The social or family situation is complex, and a mix of factors needs to be assessed before help can be provided.

— The child, adult or family has difficulty building trusting relationships but they need skilled help from a worker who is able to win their trust.

— A social situation contains clear risks to a child or adult, there is uncertainty about the best form of action to take, and both taking action and not taking action could have serious consequences

— Assessing risks and responses is made harder by unpredictable factors like family conflict or emotional stress.

— The child, adult or family may put themselves or others at risk of harm and a response has to balance the individual's interests and the well-being of others.

— The child's, adult's or family's living conditions, finances, behaviour or other circumstances are causing problems and likely to result in social exclusion.

— The behaviour of a child, adult or family causes concern or is unacceptable to neighbours or society, but evidence for action is not clear.

— The child, adult or family is facing serious difficulties, choices, bereavement, loss or other major changes which they need help and support to manage.

— The person's aspirations and needs are such that a creative approach is required to help them find or devise the solutions that are right for them.

— A disaster or emergency creates a need for urgent, wide-ranging support for victims.

Social Work Skill and Expertise

Some social work roles and tasks are identified in legislation and guidance. These include:

— Carrying accountability for decisions about whether to use legal powers or initiate emergency protection procedures

— Making judgements on whether a child or adult at risk needs to be removed to a place of safety, or whether an alternative approach would prevent the need for compulsory action.

— Being the social worker for a child in care, responsible on behalf of the local authority for carrying out the duties of the corporate parent and ensuring the child's health, wellbeing and educational progress.

— Working with children and families involved in court proceedings, both civil and criminal.

— Making joint assessments of social and nursing needs in conjunction with disabled and older people

— Cooperating with other disciplines in implementing the frameworks for inter-agency and multi-disciplinary working in children's and adults' services.

In a few instances, legislation or guidance stipulates that a role should be performed only by a social worker, or names social work as one of the professions approved for particular roles. The Independent Reviewing Officer who monitors the progress and care plans of children in care must be an experienced social worker. Social workers may be approved mental health professionals under mental health legislation, or carry out "best interests" assessments when a person may be deprived of their liberty under the Mental Capacity Act.

In other circumstances, it is the responsibility of employers to determine which situations require the deployment of a registered social worker, who may work as part of a team with social care workers and other professionals. It is recommended that an experienced social worker should always be involved in situations where:

— Investigation and action may be needed to safeguard a child or vulnerable adult from abuse, neglect, or exploitation.
— Risks must be assessed and responses planned when a child or vulnerable adult may cause significant harm to themselves or other people.
— There may be a need to remove a child from their parents or carers, or an adult from their home to a place of safety
— There is serious likelihood of family disintegration or relationship breakdown which threatens to impair health and wellbeing
— Parents or carers are unable to look after their children
— A child is in care, whether for a period or on a continuing basis
— A person is in need of support or care but unable to exercise mental capacity or provide informed consent
— The child's or vulnerable adult's future home, care or custody arrangements are disputed.
— People are being assessed as foster parents or adopters

Outcomes of Social Work

Social work aims to enable people to overcome problems and achieve the outcomes they want, in line with the Children's Plan and Putting People First. These outcomes typically include:

— More control for people over their own lives and the decisions which affect them
— Economic and financial wellbeing and a decent standard of living
— Ability to exercise human and civil rights and be active citizens
— Family stability and opportunities for children to thrive and achieve their potential
— Secure and stable alternatives for children and young people unable to stay with their families

— Safety and freedom for children and adults of all ages from abuse, harassment and discrimination
— Presence in the community for people whatever their disability, and access to the same opportunities as everyone else
— Ability to maintain or recover independence, solve practical problems and enjoy the rights and benefits of independent living
— Reduction of risks to people's physical, mental and emotional health and wellbeing, including people providing care and support to relatives and friends
— Choice of living and support arrangements for people to match their requirements and preferences
— Timely access to high quality support and care that adapts to people's changing needs and circumstances
— Ability to remain in their own home as long as possible, and not be obliged to enter institutional care unless this is their choice

Knowledge, Values and Skills

Initial social work education and training should equip people with the distinctive combination of knowledge, values and skills, drawn from a range of academic disciplines and practice learning, they require for beginning practice These include;

— Respect for the equality, worth and human rights of all people, and for their individuality, privacy and dignity
— Understanding of, and commitment to, the rights of the child
— Commitment to putting into practice equalities and diversity principles, recognising and dismantling barriers, and challenging discrimination against people using services, carers, families and fellow-workers
— Skills in assessing, jointly with people and families, their circumstances, strengths, needs and preferred outcomes
— Understanding of individual, family and community dynamics
— Skills and knowledge to deal with hostile and aggressive responses to social work intervention, without putting their own safety at risk

— Knowledge of the frameworks of law, policy and regulation affecting social work practice
— Skills, knowledge and judgement required to recognise and evaluate levels of risk to children and adults, assess possible measures to reduce and manage the risks, and take appropriate action
— Skills in enabling people to exercise choice, be involved in decisions affecting them, and use resources to secure the outcomes they want
— Skills in communication, particularly with and on behalf of children and adults with limited ability to convey their own views and wishes
— Skills in negotiating and coordinating services provided by networks of social care staff and family carers
— Skills in inter-agency collaboration and multi-disciplinary teamwork, and understanding of the roles and functions of other professions and agencies
— Information-sharing, negotiating and advocacy skills to assist people in obtaining resources, services and benefits
— Skills in effective record-keeping and use of records to review progress and learn from practice
— Commitment to continuing personal and professional development and the acquisition of advanced and specialist skills and knowledge

Knowledge-base for Practice

Drawing on a range of academic disciplines, formal research, feedback from people using services, and the experience and reflection of social workers and supervisors, a body of evidence is developing about what works well in social work, in what circumstances, for which groups of people. This knowledge is feeding into more sophisticated frameworks for evaluating complex situations, considering options and selecting methods of known effectiveness.

People using services and front-line practitioners are developing research skills and taking a larger part in defining research questions, conducting research and interpreting the results. Shared knowledge is an important tool for increasing the independence and control of people using services, and their influence over how social work is practiced and services designed.

Social Work Methods and Approaches

Methods of working in social work have evolved over a long period, rooted in common core principles but reflecting changing legal and policy frameworks, social attitudes and expectations, and relationships between professionals and the public. Key features include:

- Professional relationships based on warmth, trust and rapport with people using services
- Social models of assessing people's situations and working with them to overcome barriers to participation and independence;
- Practice that seeks to put power in the hands of people to manage their own situations, with the social worker as facilitator
- Work that integrates individual, family and community dimensions in a creative balance
- Distinctive approaches to understanding and working with risk, recognising the need to safeguard those who are vulnerable whilst enabling people to take the risks that go with ordinary everyday living
- Modern approaches to established casework skills and methodologies, working systematically and in an integrated way to keep a focus on people's practical, social and psychological wellbeing
- Applying and extending principles of personalisation, which have always been at the heart of social work at its best, to help people find individual solutions to their situations and achieve satisfactory outcomes
- Effective joint working with other disciplines, other social care staff, volunteers, foster parents and advocates

Tasks of Social Work

In order to undertake the roles described, and support people to fulfil their potential and achieve their chosen outcomes, social workers perform a variety of tasks. Not all of them are exclusive to social work, but social workers carry them out as an integral part of enabling people to achieve the outcomes they want. Some tasks are specific to work with adults, or with children and families. Often, both the children and the adults in a family need help or support, and the social worker has to be competent to understand and work with both children and adults.

Some of the principal tasks undertaken by social workers include:

— Building relationships with people who need support, winning their trust and finding good ways of communicating with them
— Working with the person or family who needs support to help them assess their situation, decide what they want to achieve, overcome barriers, and obtain support that feels right for them
— Aiding people who wish to do so to assess their own needs, identify resources, make decisions, and arrange and manage their own support
— Providing or arranging advocacy for people who do not have a voice, and helping them to be more in control of their own lives
— Acting as broker to obtain the support people want, developing creative approaches to the use of all available resources to extend individual choices, avoiding the trap of making people fit the services available, and being sensitive to unspoken needs
— Helping parents develop the skills and understanding to be more effective in meeting their children's needs for care, development and control
— Supporting the physical, intellectual and emotional development of children and young people who need help, and helping disadvantaged people of all ages improve their health and wellbeing
— Arranging good-quality alternative care for children and young people whose parents cannot care for them, and for adults who can no longer manage in their own homes

— Helping children and adults to overcome the problems of disability, negotiate the transition to adulthood and achieve independent living, access direct payments, individual budgets and other funding, and secure personal assistance, equipment and employment adjustments
— Helping people in poverty to improve their financial position, informing them about their entitlements, and supporting them to access training, work opportunities and benefits
— Regularly reviewing with people how well support fits their changing needs, involving them in co-recording progress and concerns, and agreeing adjustments and plans for ending contact
— Enabling people who are dissatisfied with the services they receive, including social work services, to make use of representations and complaints systems to seek explanations, apologies and redress
— Helping to ensure that public resources are allocated and any charges applied fairly, and informing commissioners of any evidence that the type, scale or quality of services is not matching needs.
— Seeking to promote social justice by challenging neglect, discrimination and exclusion, and helping to build safe, strong and caring social networks and communities
— Encouraging integrated working with social care workers, with other professions and agencies, with networks run by people using services, and with community support groups to improve the way services are coordinated and to better understand one another's roles

Not all the tasks arising in the course of working with a child, adult or family require the full expertise of a social worker. Social work tasks with children and families and with adults may be shared between social workers and assistants, support or care workers with the appropriate skills. New roles are emerging, supported by new forms of training, and it is possible for others to undertake and perhaps specialise in tasks which have traditionally been parts of the social work role. The social worker should retain case responsibility and a coordinating and supervisory role, to maintain integrated support and accountability.

At the same time, a clear message from children in care and other people using services is that they place a high value on continuity and consistency in their relationships with their social workers, and find constant changes of personnel a particular problem.

WORKING WITH OTHER PROFESSIONS

Social work works closely with other professional disciplines, including the various nursing specialisms, teaching, occupational therapy and other health professions, psychology, counselling, medical consultants and general practitioners, early years workers, police, youth justice and offender services. Multi-disciplinary teams have increased in number and variety in children's and adults' services, as a means of giving people access to a range of expertise, improving coordination and making best use of scarce professional skills. It is sometimes necessary to be flexible about boundaries so as to avoid people being referred unnecessarily from one source of help to another, and having to give the same information to different workers. Social work has a tradition of not sticking rigidly to professional or agency boundaries where greater flexibility serves people's best interests.

Social work should be clear and confident about the expertise it has developed, the distinctive contribution it makes and the features of its work particularly valued by people who use its services. It also has a responsibility to feed its knowledge, values and approaches into the work of joint teams to inform their culture and widen their frame of reference. Social workers who are outposted still need access to good professional supervision, learning and development opportunities, up-to-date knowledge support and links to relevant policy and practice developments.

Organisations of people using services and carers should find it useful to support their participation in service and practice review and development, and in informing the expectations of individuals and families in receipt of social work services. It has messages for work to develop the qualification and post-qualifying frameworks for social work education and training, for reviewing national occupational standards and the social work degree.

REFERENCES

Howard, M. O.,&Jenson, J. M. (2001, January). *Guidelines for social work intervention in substance abuse*. Paper presented at the 2001 Annual Conference of the Society for SocialWork and Research, Atlanta, Georgia.

Raffoul P. R. &McNeese C.A. (Eds.), *Future issues for social work practice* (pp. 270-292). Boston: Allyn & Bacon.

Reamer, F. G. (1995). Malpractice claims against social workers: First facts. *Social Work, 40*, 595-60.

Reid, W. J., & Fortune, A. E. (in press). Harbingers, origins, and approximations of evidencebased practice in current social work knowledge. In A. Rosen & E. K. Proctor (Eds.), *Developing* practice guidelines for social work interventions: Issues, methods, and research *agenda*. New York: Columbia University Press.

Bibliography

Agnew, Elizabeth N. (2004). *From Charity to Social Work: Mary E. Richmond and the Creation of an American Profession*. Urbana, IL: University of Illinois Press.

Axinn, June and Mark J. Stern (2008). *Social Welfare: A History of the American Response to Need* (7th ed.). Boston, MA: Pearson/Allyn and Bacon.

Balgopal, Pallassana R. (2000). *Social Work Practice with Immigrants and Refugees*. New York, NY: Columbia University Press.

Barker, Richard (2009). *Making Sense of Every Child Matters - multi professional practice guidance* (1st ed.). Bristol, UK: Policy Press. Riessman, C. K. (2001) 'Personal Troubles as Social Issues: A Narrative of Infertility in Context', in I. Shaw and N. Gould (eds) *Qualitative Research in Social Work: Method and Context*, pp. 73–82. Newbury Park, CA: Sage.

Butler, Ian and Gwenda Roberts (2004). *Social Work with Children and Families: Getting into Practice* (2nd ed.). London, England; New York, NY: Jessica Kingsley Publishers.

Davies, Martin (2002). *The Blackwell Companion of Social Work* (2nd ed.). Oxford, UK; Malden, MA: Blackwell.

DeRubeis, R. J., & Crits-Christoph, P. (1998). Empirically supported individual and group psychological treatments for adult mental disorders. *Journal of Consulting and Clinical Psychology, 66*, 37-52.

Evidence-Based MedicineWorking Group. (1992). Evidence-based medicine: A new approach to teaching the practice of medicine. *Journal of the American Medical Association, 268*, 2420-2425.

Fischer, J. (1976). *Effectiveness of social casework*. Springfield, IL: Charles C Thomas.

Fischer, Joel and Kevin J. Corcoran (2007). *Measures for Clinical Practice and Research: A Sourcebook* (4th ed.). Oxford, UK; New York, NY: Oxford University Press.

Foa, E. B., Keane, T. M., & Friedman, M. J. (2000). *Effective treatments for PTSD: Practice guidelines fromthe International Society for Traumatic Stress Studies*.NewYork: Guilford.

Greene, Roberta R. (2008). *Social Work with the Aged and their Families* (3rd ed.). New Brunswick, NJ: Transaction Publishers.

Grinnell, Richard M. and Yvonne A Unrau (2008). *Social Work Research and Evaluation: Foundations of Evidence-Based Practice* (8th ed.). Oxford, UK; New York, NY: Oxford University Press.

Howard, M. O.,&Jenson, J. M. (2001, January). *Guidelines for social work intervention in substance abuse*. Paper presented at the 2001 Annual Conference of the Society for SocialWork and Research, Atlanta, Georgia.

Lillrank, A. (2003) 'Back Pain and the Resolution of Diagnostic Uncertainty in Illness Narratives', *Social Science and Medicine* 57(6): 1045–54.

Maxwell, J. A. (1992) 'Understanding and Validity in Qualitative Research', *Harvard Educational Review* 62(3): 279–300.

Mishler, E. G. (1995) 'Models of Narrative Analysis: A Typology', *Journal of Narrative and Life History* 5(2): 87–123.

Mizrahi, Terry and Larry E. Davis (2008). *Encyclopedia of Social Work* (20th ed.). Washington, DC; Oxford, UK; New York, NY: NASW Press and Oxford University Press.

Popple, Philip R. and Leslie Leighninger (2008). *The Policy-Based Profession: An Introduction to Social Welfare Policy Analysis for Social Workers* (4th ed.). Boston, MA: Pearson/Allyn and Bacon.

Raffoul P. R. &McNeese C.A. (Eds.), *Future issues for social work practice* (pp. 270-292). Boston: Allyn & Bacon.

Reamer, Frederic G. (2006). *Ethical Standards in Social Work: A Review of the NASW Code of Ethics* (2nd ed.). Washington, DC: NASW Press.

Richardson, Virginia E. and Amanda Smith Barusch (2006). *Gerontological Practice for the Twenty-First Ccentury: A Social Work Perspective*. New York, NY: Columbia University Press.

Reid, W. J., & Fortune, A. E. (in press). Harbingers, origins, and approximations of evidencebased practice in current social work knowledge. In A. Rosen & E. K. Proctor (Eds.), *Developing* practice guidelines for social work interventions: Issues, methods, and research *agenda*. New York: Columbia University Press.

Riessman, C. K. (ed.) (1994) *Qualitative Studies in Social Work Research*. Thousand Oaks, CA: Sage.

Shaw, I. and Gould,N. (eds) (2001) *Qualitative Research in Social Work: Method and Context*. Newbury Park, CA: Sage.

Sowers, Karen M. and Catherine N. Dulmus and others. (2008). *Comprehensive Handbook of Social Work and Social Welfare*. Hoboken, NJ: John Wiley & Sons.

Specht, Harry; Courtney, Mark E. (1994). *Unfaithful angels : how social work has abandoned its mission*. New York: Free Press.

Statham, Daphne (2004). *Managing Front Line Practice in Social Work*. New York, NY: Jessica Kingsley Publishers.

Thomas, K. W. and Velthouse, B. A. (1990) Cognitive Elements of Empowerment: An 'Interpretive' Model of Intrinsic Task Motivation. *Academy of Management Review*, Vol 15, No. 4, 666-681.

Thyer, Bruce A. and John S. Wodarski (2007). *Social Work in Mental Health: An Evidence-Based Approach*. Hoboken, NJ: John Wiley.

Turner, Francis J. (2005). *Canadian Encyclopedia of Social Work*. Waterloo, ON: Wilfrid Laurier University Press.

Urek, M. (2005) 'Making a Case in Social Work: The Construction of an Unsuitable Mother', *Qualitative Social Work* 4(4): 451–67.

White, S. and Featherstone,B. (2005) 'Communicating Misunderstandings: Multi-agency Work as Social Practice', *Child and Family Social Work* 10: 207–16.

Wilkinson, A. 1998. *Empowerment: theory and practice. Personnel Review.* [online]. Vol. 27, No. 1, 40-56. Available from: Emerald on the World Wide Web.

Wittenberg, Renee (2003). *Opportunities in Social Work Careers* (Revised ed.). Chicago, IL: VGM Career Books.

Index